Praise for *From Where I Stand*

"*From Where I Stand* is a must-read book for all Canadians. Puglaas shares a clear understanding of where we have come from, the issues we must address, and the pathways to a transformed future. Having witnessed her remarkable courage and capacity as Canada's Attorney General and her determination to do what is right without succumbing to unrelenting political pressure, Puglaas stands tall among Canadians as a person for whom truth, thoughtfulness, and principle are not mere words – but values to sustain a different kind of policy and politics."

> MARY ELLEN TURPEL-LAFOND (AKI-KWE), *Professor of Law,*
> *Peter A. Allard School of Law, and Director of the Indian Residential School*
> *History and Dialogue Centre, University of British Columbia*

"Canadians came to understand Jody Wilson-Raybould's passion and commitment for judicial and political reform through her work as the federal Minister of Justice. Behind her engagement in the cut and thrust of politics, however, lay one of the country's most informed and thoughtful minds. In this much-anticipated book, Wilson-Raybould explains the cultural and historical roots of Indigenous hurt, anger, and despair. But true to her nature, she also offers the country a practical, reasonable, and viable path towards real and lasting reconciliation. This is a brilliant view of what is both possible and necessary."

> KEN COATES, *Canada Research Chair in Regional Innovation, and co-author of*
> From Treaty Peoples to Treaty Nation: A Road Map for All Canadians

"Jody Wilson-Raybould's quest for justice has long driven her work. I first saw this when she was a law student, and this commitment to justice has only been deepened by subsequent public service. Her unwavering commitment to reconciliation, balance, and good governance springs off every page of this book."

> JOHN BORROWS, *Canada Research Chair in Indigenous Law, Faculty of Law,*
> *University of Victoria*

"Writing from both the Big House and the House on Parliament Hill, Jody Wilson-Raybould offers unique and profound perspectives from two worlds. In this book, she maps out how First Nations can overcome the struggles of the colonial world and move toward a self-determined future in a world that is better for all. Jody's vision is clear, and her voice is essential for understanding the urgency needed for colonial and First Nations governments to develop both the political will and the commitment to action needed for a better Canada."

> TERRY TEEGEE, *Regional Chief, British Columbia Assembly of First Nations*

"JWR is on target. This must-read book speaks about our journey to an Indigenous Quiet Revolution."

> GHISLAIN PICARD, *Regional Chief, Assembly of First Nations Quebec and Labrador*

Jody Wilson-Raybould

FROM WHERE I STAND

Rebuilding Indigenous Nations
for a Stronger Canada

With a foreword by
The Honourable Murray Sinclair

PURICH
BOOKS

28 27 26 25 24 23 22 21 20 19   5 4 3 2

Printed in Canada on FSC-certified ancient-forest-free paper
(100% post-consumer recycled) that is processed chlorine- and acid-free.

Cataloguing data available from Library and Archives Canada.

ISBN 978-0-7748-8053-4 / softcover
ISBN 978-0-7748-8054-1 / EPDF
ISBN 978-0-7748-8055-8 / EPUB
ISBN 978-0-7748-8056-5 / Kindle

Canadä

UBC Press gratefully acknowledges the financial support for our publishing program
of the Government of Canada (through the Canada Book Fund),
the Canada Council for the Arts, and the British Columbia Arts Council.

Printed and bound in Canada by Friesens
Interior design: Irma Rodriguez
Set in Caslon and Fournier by Artegraphica Design Co. Ltd.
Copy editor: Lesley Erickson
Proofreader: Frank Chow
Indexer: Cheryl Lemmens
Cover designer: Will Brown
Cover art: John Henderson

Purich Books, an imprint of UBC Press
2029 West Mall
Vancouver, BC, V6T 1Z2
www.purichbooks.ca

For TJR

CONTENTS

FOREWORD

I was once asked by a young Indigenous person for advice about something they were thinking about doing: running for council in their home community. I sensed that they wanted to know what they should think about before making a decision. I said this:

> If you want to be a good leader, you have to love the people. You have to be willing to speak with a strong voice about what they need and want, and you have to do so with courage. You have to strive to understand what they are trying to tell you so you can be their voice. You have to be willing to help them understand why some things they seek cannot be achieved. You must understand that you can only lead from the front and not from the rear.

Leadership is what Jody Wilson-Raybould – Puglaas – represents for me. She is a woman who speaks her mind – her truth – with authority.

She comes from a long tradition of strong women, including her grandmother Pugladee, and was born into a family of Indigenous leaders. As a little girl she watched her father – Hemas Kla-Lee-Lee-Kla – and his colleagues publicly debate with the political leaders of Canada about the place of Aboriginal and Treaty Rights in the Constitution. She went on to law school and practised law as a representative of the Crown. She was selected by the Chiefs of BC to represent them in the Assembly of First Nations. She then went into federal politics, was elected as an MP, and was immediately appointed to cabinet as the Minister of Justice and Attorney General of Canada, where she exercised influence on important issues.

Jody Wilson-Raybould was not only born to be a leader but accepted the role as her responsibility, and she has fulfilled it with honour and grace and courage. There is no one better-suited to reflect on the shared future of Canada and what needs to be done to make reconciliation a reality in this country. *From Where I Stand* is based on speeches made during her time as BC Regional Chief and Minister of Justice and Attorney General, speeches informed by her cultural teachings, upbringing, and her lived experience. They reflect Jody's thoughts on tradition, leadership, law, history, colonialism, constitutionalism, governance, feminism, and politics and the important role that they have played and will continue to play in Indigenous Nation building.

This book makes an important contribution to the process of reconciliation. Whatever you might or might not agree with in its pages, it will make you think, react, and – hopefully – act. To make reconciliation a reality, we must have important conversations, and for the past ten years Jody has added her voice on issues that matter the most, including the Indian Act, Indigenous Rights, and the duty to consult. As you read this book, you won't be able to get away with dismissing her thoughts and ideas – even if you sometimes feel they raise more questions that need answers. And isn't that what all good books should do – provoke conversations and debates – especially at this crucial time in the reconciliation process?

When we completed the *Truth and Reconciliation Final Report*, I was aware that Canadian society was entering a new era of discourse about reconciliation. And as a judge and Senator, I knew that governments, Indigenous Peoples, and individuals would all need to work together to translate this greater understanding into concrete action. Emerging understandings and definitions of reconciliation will need to take shape in tangible ways in the lives of individuals, communities, and our country as a whole, and this book helps show us the way.

Reconciliation means we need to create a future together that best comes to terms with our past. Jody's words will help us do it right and do it together.

Senator Murray Sinclair
Winnipeg, Manitoba
August 2019

From Where I Stand

INTRODUCTION

A central lesson instilled in me from a very young age was to be careful with words because you cannot take them back – you must always speak the truth. This has been a vital teaching and one that has guided me in my relationships, as I strive to always be thoughtful and considerate in working with others.

It has guided me in how I have approached the various roles I have been fortunate to play, including as a Crown prosecutor in Vancouver from 2000 to 2003, as Regional Chief of the Assembly of First Nations for British Columbia from October 2009 to June 2015, and as the first Member of Parliament for the new riding of Vancouver Granville from October 2015 to the present. And it guided me when I was subsequently appointed the first Indigenous Minister of Justice and Attorney General of Canada, from November 2015 to January 2019.

In these roles and others, I have given numerous speeches and lectures. Preparing for speeches and lectures is not a task I take lightly. It is a privilege, but moreover, it is a responsibility when speaking on matters where there is urgency in people's lives and when the words you say might have a substantive impact. While I have people to assist me and to review drafts, I spend hours upon hours writing and editing draft after draft, trying to ensure that every word is as it should be. Indeed, as those who have worked with me would attest, right up until the moment I give my remarks I am rewriting parts to make sure I am being appropriately careful with the words I use.

Giving speeches and lectures has given me the opportunity to reflect, in a systematic way, on the Indigenous-Crown relationship and the future of Canada, and I have done so from the unique perspective of having been both an advocate for Indigenous Peoples (as Regional Chief) and then the chief law officer of Canada (as Minister of Justice and Attorney General). This book is based on my speeches, lectures, committee evidence, and other writings on Indigenous issues – all from over the course of the last ten years. Front and centre in all these writings is the challenge of reconciliation and Indigenous empowerment – of Nation rebuilding – addressing Canada's colonial legacy and building a future where Indigenous Rights are recognized, respected, and fully implemented. This is the work that we need to do as a country if we are to reach our full potential. And, to be sure, it is a responsibility for all of us. As individuals, businesses, governments, faith-based organizations, and civil society, we all have vital roles to play along with Indigenous Peoples – First Nations, Métis, and Inuit – and their governments. Reconciliation touches on all aspects of our shared future: how we build ever greater social, cultural, economic, environmental, and political well-being and how we achieve balance as a society.

Creating a more just and equal Canada characterized by transformed relations with Indigenous Peoples is a deeply personal matter for me – it is the work I was raised to be a part of. In lighthearted moments, people might hear me refer to myself as "just a little Indian girl from a small fishing village on an island off the west coast of British Columbia." But when I say this, it is actually expressing much about the multigenerational reality of who I am, and where I come from, and why I approach the work of reconciliation the way I do.

I come from the Musgamagw Tsawateineuk/Laich-Kwil-Tach people of northern Vancouver Island, who are part of the Kwakwaka'wakw, also known as the Kwak'wala-speaking peoples. Our culture, worldview, spirituality, and way of life are integrally related to the natural world around us – the land, air, and waters that have always sustained us.

My society, in important ways, is a matrilineal one. This means that descent is traced and property is inherited through the female line. My grandmother's name was Pugladee – the highest-ranking name in our Clan – the Eagle Clan. Her name means "a good host" – a name that was given to my older sister, Kory, at the same time I was given my name, Puglaas. "Puglaas" means "a woman born to noble people." These names were given in a naming Potlatch at Gilford Island when I was five and my sister six. My father's name is Hemas Kla-Lee-Lee-Kla, which means "number one amongst the eagles, the Chief who is always there to help." He is our Clan's hereditary Chief.

We are "potlatching" peoples. A Potlatch is a traditional institution of governance – a central one that we still practise. It is here that our names are passed down or given from generation to generation. It is where laws are made, disputes are settled, people are married, and wealth is redistributed. In our Potlatch, the highest-ranking male leaders are called *Hamatsa*.

I am fortunate to come from a strong and loving family. My grandmother, parents, and family ensured that both my sister and I knew our culture, our values, the laws of our Big House, and how to conduct oneself as a leader. I was raised to be proud of who I am, to know where I came from, to believe in myself, and to recognize my rights and responsibilities. In our system, I am a Hiligaxste' (a role always held by women). One of my jobs is to lead my Hamatsa, the Chief, into the Big House. This role can be translated as one who "corrects the Chief's path." We show them the way – a metaphor for life. In the Potlatch, this is symbolized in our rituals when the power of the Hamatsa is "tamed" and he is ready to be Chief. In my family, it meant I was raised to lead from a very young age. My family instilled in me a sense of community and duty – that I had something to give back and to contribute, to use my skills and abilities, such as they are, to improve the quality of life for our people and others. My upbringing, my education, my professional and personal experiences have all helped shape my worldview and the way I try to conduct myself.

In my culture, holding the name "Puglaas," like other names, comes with clear expectations, responsibilities, and accountabilities. Today, this is the work of helping to carry forward, in an ever-changing world, our communitarian teachings – in which everyone has a role to play, creating a society where our people, and all peoples, can live together in patterns of harmony and unity while upholding, celebrating, and respecting the distinctiveness of diverse peoples and the beauty, strength, and knowledge they bring to our human family.

This work of reconciliation and Nation rebuilding, for myself and for many other Indigenous leaders and people, has also meant telling the history of being resilient and standing firm in the face of colonization and oppression. While we know the true history of Canada is increasingly being understood, it continues to require retelling, re-examination, and reinterpretation. Indeed, and thankfully, young Canadians today grow up knowing about residential schools, missing and murdered Indigenous women and girls, the Indian Act, and the violation of the basic human rights of Indigenous Peoples. They also are increasingly aware that the legacy of colonization remains with us, seen in the significant socioeconomic gaps that still exist between Indigenous and non-Indigenous peoples across Canada. The fact that this true history has come to light, and that its legacy today is increasingly understood, is a testament to how Indigenous parents, grandparents, great-grandparents, and others persevered, fought, and advocated over many decades.

We truly have come a long way. Even a decade ago, when the first speeches in this book were being prepared, Canadian society at large was not as broadly conversant about reconciliation. Many governments were passively disinterested, positive media stories were more rare than common, artists and authors creating insights about the Indigenous reality were on the margins, and it was harder to get industry into the room. In substantive ways, all of these former realities have changed or are changing. As a country, we are increasingly engaged in the work of reconciliation, and progressive steps are being taken. We are moving from a learning moment to an action moment. We do, indeed, live in interesting and exciting times.

But the optimism comes with a warning. Expectations are high; we are not there yet. We must capitalize on the momentum to ensure that progress continues – to take advantage of it. This can be a real challenge because sincere intent leads to genuine action, which drives change, and change is hard to implement and sustain. While people often talk about the need for change, actually making it happen is something else. And to be clear, the changes that reconciliation brings are, and will be, significant. They touch on all dimensions of our public and private lives, including how governments make decisions, how economies function, how children are educated, how our justice system operates and is structured, and how our environment is cared for. It is hard work. And not surprisingly, as individuals, we are often confused about what we should be doing. Indeed, in speaking with Canadians across the country, the two questions I am most often asked are "What can I do?" and "How can I make a difference?"

While individual Canadians are acting and seeking further direction on the constructive steps they can take, within government one confronts the challenge of how to shift course when things have been focused in another direction for so long and patterns of behaviour so engrained. The analogy I often use is that government is like a massive ship that has been heading through the ocean in one way for 150 years. Our task now is to turn that ship and send it off in another direction. I know government systems are not designed to adjust course quickly, and politicians tend to bias the near term, focusing on electoral cycles and prospects. And this is why we must move beyond partisanship: to set and keep the course so that, in time, the ship will inevitably turn.

This analogy can also apply to Indigenous Peoples, Nations, and their evolving governments. In many respects, Indigenous Peoples have become accustomed to patterns that have been imposed upon us, including, for First Nations, having our lives controlled and administered by the Indian Act. In the fog created by layers upon layers of colonial imposition – including multiple generations being told that, as "Indians," they are nothing more than numbers, with identity cards, whose lives and well-being are subject to a system of band administration on a reserve – it is sometimes hard to know what the future could look like and to set the course on how to get there.

In my speeches, I often refer to this as navigating our way through the "postcolonial door" – a separate but similar analogy we developed at the BC Assembly of First Nations to illustrate a continuum of governance reform and of Nation rebuilding. Represented visually by three doors – one

locked, one partially open, and one fully opened to a new future based on self-determination – the analogy refers to the fact that opening the door will require the Crown, in partnership with Indigenous Peoples, to remove legislative, policy, and other barriers to Indigenous Nation rebuilding in Canada. It will also require Indigenous Peoples to actually engage in the hard work of rebuilding to open the door and navigate through it. In the oft-cited words of the Supreme Court of Canada, "we are all here to stay," and building a shared postcolonial future will depend on us working together while enabling Indigenous Nations to determine their own course.

For Indigenous Peoples the challenge of breaking out of entrenched patterns becomes heightened and very real as the federal government actually changes its course – as it moves from denial and to rights recognition and support for true Nation rebuilding. When real change is happening or on the horizon, Indigenous Peoples need to set their own internal course to arrive at a future place where their priorities and visions lead the way. What is encouraging is that all across the country and within our evolving system of cooperative federalism, Indigenous Peoples are exercising their right to self-determination – lifting the fog in different ways and at different paces, striving to emerge into the future they wish to see. They are setting their own internal course to a place where, ultimately, Indigenous govern-

The Three Doors

ments and Nations will be rebuilt, where they will be self-governing over their lands and resources and caring for the well-being of their citizens and others within their jurisdiction. Which raises the question: Has the federal ship's course correction truly been made to support this work? If not, what more needs to be done? What are the course-setting or course-correcting solutions?

While the work is hard – even daunting at times – the good news is that we have the solutions. We know what must be done. For decades now, we have had studies, reports, and analyses that have identified the paths forward, including the work that must be done by Indigenous Peoples, governments, industry, and the general public. We also have decades of Indigenous Peoples advocating and charting the course forward and building approaches to a new future. We do not need more studies. My message has always been, and continues to be, that it is time to act because we know what actions are needed. We all know what needs to be done but we need to have the courage and the conviction to do it.

In their own way, this is what all the speeches and writings in this book set out to do – to provide a frame for a course correction for both government and Indigenous Peoples – to open a path to correct and stay the course, so to speak, and to lift the fog. While they were completed over the span of almost a decade, their core purpose and themes have remained the same. Importantly, as should be clear in reading them, there is no distance between the themes and ideas I developed and explored in speeches when I was Regional Chief and those I delivered when I was Minister of Justice and Attorney General of Canada. While some of the niceties and nuances may read differently, the messages are the same.

The speeches and writings all, in some way, speak to the message of Nation rebuilding and empowering Indigenous Peoples within an even stronger Canadian federation. They speak to the course we should be setting to get there. They all express how relations with Indigenous Peoples in this country are transforming and must continue to transform. And they include stories of listening, learning, and reflection. At times they speak to feelings of frustration. Indeed, some of the most blunt and frank calling out of government misunderstanding or inaction is from my time as minister, when I had to confront the challenge of moving from rhetoric to action from the inside and push for real change. But they ultimately convey a narrative of hope and optimism: that change is occurring, that we are close to being on course, that what is required is renewed vision and leadership.

Collectively, and the way they are presented here, the speeches explore five broad themes that offer a foundational understanding of the challenge of reconciliation in Canada today. One of these themes is the meaning of reconciliation itself – why we have come to use that term and what it might mean. Both at home and abroad, this was perhaps the topic I was asked and am asked to speak about more than any other. I was honoured to be the first non-Australian lecturer to give the Annual Reconciliation Lecture in Canberra in 2016, and I used my time there to talk about how understanding and defining reconciliation today requires examining Canada's history and the stories we tell ourselves. At the heart of this is recognizing that the Indian Act – truly "colonial" legislation, in all the negative senses of that term – imposed and structured a form of race-based oppression within our own country. When I spoke to the Assembly of First Nations in 2013 on the sad occasion of the death of Nelson Mandela, I similarly compared colonialism in Canada to the experience of other countries and argued that reconciliation involves rising through our own unique challenges to move through the postcolonial door.

In Canada, this requires understanding and honouring our unique Constitution, which includes recognition and protection for Indigenous Rights, including Treaty Rights, a second theme I explore in depth in my speeches. Section 35 recognized and affirmed these rights in 1982 – but these rights were not created in 1982. Indigenous Rights are inherent, a result of the fact that Indigenous Peoples owned and governed the lands and resources that now make up Canada prior to the arrival of Europeans. The challenge we must face as part of reconciliation is that these rights have been denied – they have not been upheld and implemented. Section 35 of our Constitution, as well as the United Nations Declaration on the Rights of Indigenous Peoples (UNDRIP), are legal instruments designed to address and overcome this denial. But, for the most part, Crown governments still require Indigenous Peoples to "prove" their rights, and their denial has for far too long been used as a justification for doing little or nothing to assist Indigenous Peoples to move beyond the colonial legacy. My speeches address what we actually need to do to recognize and implement rights, to make UNDRIP workable domestically, including Canada's need for a comprehensive rights recognition and implementation framework to help lay the foundations for governance in a post-Indian Act world, my third theme.

Indigenous Peoples have roles and responsibilities they must play in rebuilding their governments and Nations, but, as I argued in my address to the First Nations–Crown Gathering in 2012, before we can concentrate on the hard work of Nation rebuilding, we need to topple the Indian Act tree and develop mechanisms to let strong and appropriate institutions, structures, and procedures of governance grow in its place. Spoiler alert – while some may be critical of Indigenous Peoples for the quality of governance on reserve under the Indian Act, it is not Indigenous Peoples' fault that the Indian Act system does not work. Indeed, nowhere around the globe have colonial, authoritarian, arbitrary, and paternalistic models of government proven to be effective, efficient, particularly workable, or desirable. There are, of course, many ways to govern, but what matters most is that it is legitimate and done well. Self-determination, including self-government, is the answer and has been a central component of my vision since I became Regional Chief and advanced the "Building on OUR Success" action plan, which included a Governance Toolkit to help

maintain balance in Canada. Questions about what constitutes balance and how we can achieve it, whether within the justice system or in ensuring gender equality, are complex, and they are conversations that need to continue.

To be honest, though, prior to entering federal politics, I never fully considered what it meant to be a feminist or if, indeed, I considered myself a feminist in the sense or ways that the term is often used today. As a Kwakwaka'wakw woman, my roles and responsibilities have always been clear to me and the values of equality, freedom, respect, inclusion, and upholding each other emphasized. But being an Indigenous woman in federal politics has caused me to reflect a lot on questions of gender equality, diversity, and balance and, in so doing, to see parallels between my personal experience and the historical and ongoing struggle of Indigenous Peoples in this country.

I was compelled to resign from cabinet on a matter of principle in February 2019 and was subsequently removed from the Liberal caucus. This experience made me see more clearly than ever that Ottawa, politics, and its modes of functioning maintain norms and patterns that are not always compatible with my culture, my worldview, or my gender. For sure, society has changed, and politics have changed. And we can be proud as Canadians because of this. But Canadian society has still not changed nearly enough. The work of building a society that reflect the visions, strengths, potentialities, and contributions of all of us, as Canadians, is still very much ongoing, a work in progress.

There are, of course, other aspects to understanding reconciliation, and, indeed, I reflect on many other important and vital issues in this book. As you read through it, I hope you will see the integrative nature of the challenge of reconciliation. It requires that we understand our shared history and reimagine our future; that we examine our individual attitudes and actions as well as our shared ones; that we understand our laws and legal system but not place too much emphasis on legal systems alone; that we recognize that new legislation is needed but that so, too, are basic changes in how we think, act, and relate as human beings; that we realize that both Indigenous and non-Indigenous governments have a role to play but so, too, do each of us as individuals.

As I reread my speeches in putting together this introduction, I was left with the feeling that the Canadian government lost an opportunity during the Forty-Second Parliament. Yes, progress was made on Indigenous issues. But we still cannot say with confidence that the ship's course has been shifted sufficiently to turn it in a new direction — away from denial and towards unqualified recognition, as I outlined in my speech to the BC Leadership Gathering on November 29, 2018. With courage and transformative leadership and action, more could have been done. Moving forward, my resolve to push on, to correct the course, has only been strengthened.

I initially decided to run to be a Member of Parliament for many reasons — but key among them was the desire to help create the legal and political space for Indigenous Peoples to be self-determining, including self-governing. As I have said to countless audiences in Canada and around the world, the fortunes of Canada and Indigenous Peoples are intertwined. Rebuilding Indigenous Nations will result in a stronger, better Canada, one that will enrich all Canadians. My vision has not changed. To this end, I recently spoke at an honouring ceremony in our Big House in Campbell River. I spoke about how entering mainstream politics and working in the political environment that I now do has heightened my appreciation that there is much Ottawa can learn from Indigenous Peoples, from our worldview and our societies. We have legal orders that have survived for millennia and are very much part of our evolving legal framework in Canada.

I have been honoured to play the roles I have. I acknowledge the unique vantage point that I have had, being an elected Indigenous leader and an elected federal minister of the Crown. It is a vantage point few have had in the past and undoubtedly more will have in the future. When I reflect on what I have learned, I sometimes see an image of the country emerging from darkness, to half-light, to full brightness. As Canada comes to terms with its colonial past and as Indigenous Peoples increasingly continue to determine their own futures, the full potential of this country will shine. My hope is that this book may help in some small way to inspire new visions, more light for the future, and galvanize action. There is more work to be done, and I am confident it will get done. Reconciliation cannot fail, because Canada cannot fail.

Moving through the Postcolonial Door

"

Before we can walk through the door
to a postcolonial world, we have to empower
our communities from the ground up.

"

We Truly Have Come a Long Way ...

Keynote address to the 6th Annual Western Canada
Aboriginal Law Forum, May 12, 2010

Since time lost in memory, our Nations were here and existed in sophisticated societies that were self-governing and self-sufficient. The colonial period, while just a blip along our timeline as First Nations, has been devastating. However, we are moving into a postcolonial period.

I find myself as the Regional Chief of the BC Assembly of First Nations during a time of significant change and opportunity. Your agenda and its range of topics are reflective of our Nations' current realities – how far we have come and where we are going. There is a lot of work, community development work, ahead of us to empower and strengthen our diverse Nations. We must establish a new reality in the lives of our people. We all have an important role to play during this period of removing the final vestiges of colonialism.

To this end, we truly have come a long way in the last fifty years. Fifty years ago, Canada was a long way from answering the legal question as to whether or not there was still Aboriginal Title in British Columbia. Fifty years ago, we did not know the scope and extent of the Crown's fiduciary relationship with us as Aboriginal Peoples in the wake of the colonial legacy and the assumption by the Crown of legal responsibility for our affairs. We did not know the legal extent of our Aboriginal Rights. The Canadian Constitution had not been amended to address our peoples' rights in section 35, and there were no First Nations in Canada that were recognized as "self-governing" – there were no settlements of comprehensive land claims and no comprehensive or sectoral self-government initiatives. Fifty years ago, our Provincial Territorial Organizations in British Columbia were in their infancy or did not exist at all. And, for the most part, there was no economic development on any reserves in BC, save for a handful of mobile-home parks in a couple of communities in BC. There was no Assembly of First Nations – no office of the Regional Chief. For the most part, our political voice was dispersed throughout our Nations, and compared to today we were not as organized.

Today, we are in an exciting period of change, a period of Nation building or Nation rebuilding – with opportunities our people did not have fifty years ago or could only dream of. This change has occurred due to leadership and political pressure supported by significant advances in the courts, establishing the legal principles that now guide and shape our relationship with other Canadians. In fact, fifty years ago there were no First Nations lawyers, because prior to 1951 the Indian Act defined a "person" as "an individual other than an Indian." Ten years after and with changes to the Indian Act, Hereditary Chief Alfred Scow, C.M., of the Qui'Qwa'Sot'Enox Nation on Gilford Island near Port Hardy, became the first Aboriginal person in BC to graduate from law school (UBC), in 1961, then to become a member of the bar and to be appointed to the bench.

The lawyers in the 1960s and '70s who advocated for our rights were, therefore, predominantly non-Aboriginal. The money was not lucrative, and many did it out of political and moral conviction. Fifty years ago, there were no conferences such as this and, if there had been, the agenda would have certainly been shorter and far less complicated. Fifty years ago, advocacy supported the basic recognition of Aboriginal Rights and Title. *Calder* (1973) took four days at trial. Juxtapose this with the 339 days of trial in *Tsilhqot'in Nation v British Columbia* (2007) or *Delgamuukw v British Columbia* (1997), which heard 374 days of evidence and legal argument.

A lot has changed in fifty years – legally and politically. But while some progress has been made socially in improving the lives of our people, there still remains significant distance between the quality of the lives of our people and other Canadians, this despite the advances made in recognition of our rights through the courts. So, we must ask: Why is this? And what can we do about it?

There is no question much work remains to be done in advancing Aboriginal Title and Rights and improving the lives of our people, not the least of which is actually having a court issue the first declaration of Aboriginal Title in this province. But despite the work that remains in advancing our broad rights and title issues and getting governments on side, I am going to be so bold as to suggest it is we, First Nations, who have the greatest responsibility to act on our opportunities. We are now in the driver's seat.

Two weeks ago, I was fortunate to have participated on a panel at the ninth United Nations Permanent Forum on Indigenous Issues in New York. The big news at the session was New Zealand declaring its support for the Declaration, the United States saying that they have decided to conduct a formal review of the Declaration on the Rights of Indigenous Peoples with the expectation that they would sign, and Canada indicating that they were taking steps to endorse the United Nations Declaration on the Rights of Indigenous Peoples in a manner that is fully consistent with Canada's Constitution, laws, and in a "timely manner." The United Nations Declaration is, of course, an important landmark in the advancement of Indigenous Peoples' Rights globally. It is particularly important for those countries where Indigenous Peoples remain legally, politically, and socially marginalized and where their actual existence is threatened by the state. It becomes very obvious when you participate in these forums just how far First Nations people in Canada have come in terms of addressing our issues compared to other Nations.

While I felt proud of our accomplishments, at the same time I could not help but feel somewhat guilty when it came to other Indigenous Peoples and how we represented ourselves as being in their same shoes. What did the Indigenous delegates think about Canada? For example, what did they think when they heard that the Government of Canada spends over $10 billion on Aboriginal Peoples in addition to the general government expenditure on Canadians, not taking into account provincial expenditure or the $3 billion that our Nations generate in our own revenues?

I could not help but think that for these people the United Nations Declaration probably means considerably more for their future where their rights are not recognized in their state's Constitution or where the courts simply ignore them or rule against their arguments and where there is very limited financial support. I can hear some of you thinking, *What is she saying? Is she saying she does not support the UN Declaration, or that everything is perfect in Canada, or the courts have given us all that we need?* Of course, I am not that naive. I fully support the UN Declaration, and everything is far from perfect in Canada. The courts have not given us all that we need. But what I am saying is that we have opportunities and are demonstrating our success. Our situation is certainly a lot better than what some of our political leaders from across Canada would suggest, and it is on this note that I want to turn to the issues that confront us today in BC, issues that are as much about getting our people in a position to implement their rights and empowering them as they are about advocating abstract legal concepts of Aboriginal Title and Rights.

We must work to ensure that the people who actually live in our communities can benefit directly from the advancements that we have collectively made and which we can celebrate and be proud of.

As I sat in the General Assembly Hall of the United Nations, I also could not help but wonder, *What would the average person living in our communities think about the relative merits of the endorsement of the Declaration? What would it mean to them?* For most of our people who live on reserves, I would suggest important legal covenants such as the UN Declaration – or even section 35 of the Canadian Constitution and the reams of Aboriginal Title and Rights cases flowing from it – mean very little as they personally struggle to make ends meet, as they try to make do in the backward political chaos of Indian Act government and the confused and contradictory relationships we still have with Canada as both colonial authority and a partner.

I have been trying, as I am sure many of you have been trying, to figure out what it is we need to do to empower and facilitate social change in our communities so more of our Nations are ready to move beyond the Indian Act, to where change is reflective of our Aboriginal Title and Rights and is also practical, so our people can enjoy their title and their rights, so that no one can argue that the only people who benefit from the "system" are those that get elected to council, their family, or those who work for the band or those who have chosen or have been forced to live and work away from our communities.

I would respectfully suggest that there is currently a large disconnect between the rights we have established and our ability to actually take advantage of our opportunities. We have to ask why, to ask why some of our communities are doing better than others – particularly where they have similar demographic and geographic profiles. The answer is, at least in part, due to leadership. In part it could be due to a community facing a crisis or an issue. For others, it might be because of special relationships with third parties. In all cases, I would suggest there is a level of understanding throughout those Nations' membership that there is life beyond the Indian Act and opportunities for the taking if the community is prepared and healthy enough to support social change.

In looking forward to what needs to be done to translate Aboriginal Title and Rights into benefits on the ground, we actually have to start in our communities with our people. Basic community development. This reality is actually not all that complicated or radical a thought. It is just hard to accomplish and not always politically expedient for government to support although ultimately necessary to formally end the colonial period, as I shall explain.

What I have learned in my short time in regional and national politics and working in my own community is that before there can be any significant social change on the ground in implementing our Aboriginal Title and Rights, our people have to support it, not just verbally and politically through electing leaders that share the same vision, but they actually have to exercise their franchise and vote in favour of change. They have to vote for social change. The twisted reality of our postcolonial transition is that our people have to vote the colonizer out. As you are all aware, this is because the colonizer – in our case, Canada – has a fiduciary relationship to our people and cannot simply legislate the Indian Act away until our people tell them it is okay to do so. Perverse but true.

No other segment of Canadian society had to decolonize or go through this process to establish basic structures of governance or create the tools for economic and social development. The legal framework and institutional structure for good government and creating the legislative framework to support economic development is in place for the rest of Canada, but not for us – unless we vote "yes" to change. While many of our communities have traditional systems still intact, they nevertheless remain overshadowed – at least on reserve – by the Indian Act reality. Our own people, depressingly, often hide behind that reality to their own detriment. This is not their fault.

Many of our people are very unhealthy and still suffer from postcolonial trauma, a result of the residential school experience, the establishment of the reserve system, government-defined citizenship, historical racism, and the marginalization of our economies. So how do we develop healthy communities with a well-educated and well-rounded citizenry that is sufficiently beyond the colonial experience to be able to participate in referendums and vote out a system that is suffocating? It is a bit of a chicken-and-egg situation, and this is why the work we are all involved in to support social change in our communities is so difficult and at times so unforgiving. But it is this basic community development that we must all embrace and take on the challenge with vigour – with conviction and based on principle.

When I ran for BCAFN Regional Chief, I did so with my eyes wide open. I believe I was elected because there are many leaders across BC who are open to the challenge and are fighting to open the "door" in their own communities to the opportunities we now have. I believe our leaders are concerned that despite the fact the door has now been opened, far too few of our people and our communities are being able to pass through it. To open that door fully and walk through it, we still need Canada and BC to assist us. It is still far too difficult and far too expensive and complicated for communities to navigate their way to the other side of the postcolonial door – all of which is compounded if communities are not healthy or ready to vote "yes" to change.

While it takes money to mount a movement for social change and effect social change – it is not just about money – there will never be enough money. It will take conviction, and it will take dedication, with local champions of change that understand that without such change First Nations will continue to be mired by the challenges of the colonial period. In fact, it will take all of us.

When we look at the level of resources available to our people both federally and provincially, and at our ever-increasing own sources of revenue, we need to be more efficient and more strategic in the types of investments we make in our own future. We need to ensure that Canadian and, where applicable, provincial policies support the investment in community empowerment and development. We need to take control, and we need to set the direction.

In this province, we currently have three Provincial Territorial Organizations (PTOs). The first, established in 1969, was the Union of British Columbia Indian Chiefs to address the land question. The First Nations Summit was established in 1991 to also address the land question, ostensibly through treaty making, and thirdly, the BC Assembly of First Nations, part of the national Assembly of First Nations structure. As time has passed, there is now considerable blurring between the functions and support for each of these organizations. Some First Nations belong to one, some to two, and some First Nations belong to all three of these organizations while some belong to none.

A few years back, the leadership of these organizations came together and established something called the "Leadership Council," which was supported by the membership of each of the respective organizations. For some of us, this signalled recognition that we were really coming together and planning our postcolonial strategy and how to collectively advance our Aboriginal Title and Rights. The advancements made in the duty of the Crown to consult and accommodate where there is a presumption of Aboriginal Title has really forced, in a good way, the Province of British Columbia to consider how the government can recognize our Aboriginal Rights and begin sharing in natural resource wealth through accommodation and benefits agreements. What has happened in this regard over the last year has been very interesting and informative in our struggle for social change and how we organize politically.

Last year, the Leadership Council and the provincial government through their legal teams developed a proposed Recognition and Reconciliation Act that was soundly rejected by each of the three PTOs' membership. I believe the framework for reconciliation and recognition did not properly account for the ongoing struggle at our community level and the reality that before we can walk through the door to a postcolonial world we actually have to empower our communities and our people from the ground up. The failure of the Leadership Council and the province to advance a province-wide framework for reconciliation and recognition that could be supported by the Chiefs precipitated a review of our provincial political institutions. A First Nations' Task Force was struck comprised of leaders representing the diversity of our province, and this Task Force is preparing a report for our communities to consider on the best way to politically organize ourselves moving forward.

Personally, I think that there is too much duplication of work among the three organizations. This duplication, combined with a desire by our leaders to work together as more and more of us appreciate the amount of work we each need to do in our own communities in order to be able to walk through the postcolonial door, means it is time to consider merging our political organizations. This will help us share our experiences, both good and bad, maximize our limited resources, and help each other so that the bulk of the resources can be dedicated to community development on the ground. It will be interesting to see what the Task Force proposes and how the Chiefs-in-Assembly respond to the report. I look forward to the debate.

I was elected on a platform of empowerment and community development. Our plan focuses on four key and interrelated areas. All are based upon a fundamental principle of community empowerment that assumes that at some point every community in our province will be voting to walk through the door to a postcolonial world, that each will need to develop a strategy, an exit strategy, to move beyond the Indian Act.

The first part of the plan is, not surprisingly, strong and appropriate governance. Each community – either individually or in groups, depending upon cultural and social ties and issues of proper title holder – will need to determine how they will govern themselves and build their contemporary institutions of governance. Strong and appropriate governance is truly necessary to be successful. All the academic work and experience show that if our Nations are to reach our full potential and maximize our opportunities, we need to govern ourselves appropriately. Without it, there is too much political and legal uncertainty, leading to wasted energy and money, energy and money we do not have for fights often fought locally. Basically, the dysfunction that plagues Indian Act band offices across the country needs to end.

At the BCAFN, for our part, as a political organization that supports our constituent members, we are developing what we are calling a "Governance Engagement and Self-Assessment Tool" to assist communities in developing appropriate government as part of a social change movement and to stimulate discussion, a discussion that needs to take place around our council tables, in staff meetings and, most importantly, at band meetings and around the kitchen tables of the citizens in our communities.

Our plan also includes working in the area of fair lands and resources settlements. Our communities need their own sources of revenue. There are now opportunities for revenue-sharing agreements and accommodation. We need to work towards all our communities having access to resource revenue sharing – available to all and not just those that can afford the lawyers or maybe have the political connections to engage with the Crown. It is key – fair land and resource settlements that fund the rebuilding of our societies, help pay for our governments, and help provide towards the cost of programs and services our people develop and deliver in our own communities. We need to share and help communities that may not have as easy access to the resources needed to begin to benefit from their land and resource rights.

Finally, at the BCAFN we are focusing on the individual because the collective is only as strong as the individuals that make it up. We need healthy individuals to participate in our new beginning, individuals that are free from or can deal with the trauma of the colonial experience. This is one of our biggest challenges as there is still a lot of healing required. We need to ensure that those who are entrusted to assist our communities in the healing process understand the link between healing and governance reform; the need to establish appropriate governance and how we can benefit from lands and resources settlements that we are increasingly entering into. It is all linked. Our objective is not just to treat the symptoms of colonialism but to eradicate the disease completely.

We also need individuals that are educated. There is a need to ensure we continue the progress we have made in education, not just postsecondary education but rounded in terms of their knowledge of the public policy issues we face and the important decisions our people will be asked to make in the next ten years. Our people, unlike other Canadians, are going to be asked to vote on important aspects of social change before their community can pass through the postcolonial door. If they do not understand what is being asked of them, or why, they will inevitably vote "no" to change.

This is an important point that is often overlooked. As First Nations in a wardship relationship with the Crown – part of the colonial legacy – we cannot remove the remaining shackles of colonialism until our people vote in favour, until and unless we work together to ensure that we all understand and are a part of the positive social change. This is perhaps the greatest contradiction in the relationship we have with the Crown – as both colonial authority and partner. In fact, this is such a problem some have suggested Canada ought to separate Indian Affairs into two offices – one that deals with the colonial management of reserves and one that does not. I am not sure how practical this would be, but thinking about the contradiction does highlight the legal and administrative problems we have as being both wards of the state and also peoples with an inherent right of self-government.

Those of you who work or live in our communities know what I am talking about. You recognize how challenging the local politics and the reality of our community life can be. Some of you have moved away from your community. You may go back occasionally, to visit relatives, to participate in cultural activities, maybe to work. In many cases, you probably left because of work and the opportunities that now exist for our people away from home.

But as Indigenous People we all have a home, we all have a Nation, and we all have a language and a unique culture. When many of us move to the city or take on roles outside of our community, including the professional role as a lawyer or a consultant or working for other governments, we are still participating in the building of a better future for our people but do so within a safe distance away from the reality, and often poverty, of our reserves, within the safety net of our professions and the institutions that we work for. While some pundits may criticize us – whether as politicians, lawyers, or consultants – that we are now part of an "Indian industry" enriching ourselves on the backs of the suffering of our people who live back home, I do not subscribe to this condemnation of our collective aspirations to better the lives of our people.

Having said that, it is not hard to see why the pundits, perhaps egged on by the dispossessed in our communities, have a perception of us as elites. We need to overcome this perception by ensuring our Nations are supported in their rebuilding. We all need to think like a community development worker first.

For First Nations people, I do not need to tell you how we all share a responsibility to give back to our people, and we all do so in different ways. For those of you who belong to a community, consider what it is that you are doing or could do to assist your own community in walking through the door to a postcolonial world. Perhaps not just in advocating Aboriginal Title and Rights in court, but how can you influence opinion around the kitchen tables of your reserve? Regardless of local politics and family divisions, in what ways can you safely work with those of like mind to empower your fellow citizens to move beyond the stagnation of Indian Act reality? I guess I am asking you to become part of a growing movement for social change that our people are demanding and that is founded on implementing our hard-fought struggle for Aboriginal Title and Rights so a new opportunity is not lost or only benefits a few. When citizens of one community begin to ask why another community is doing better than their community, our citizens will want answers and will want us to work together. Success begets success.

For those of you that are not First Nations, you, too, continue to have a significant role in supporting our people passing through the postcolonial door. Ask yourself what is it that your company, your business, or your legal firm – and what you individually – are already doing or can do to assist in community development work. Many of you are tireless and are passionate about what you do and spend hours working on our issues. For that, we thank you.

So I ask: What can I, as Regional Chief, do politically to help channel your collective compassion and your energy to support our community development work so that our resources and our time is maximized, so that we improve the chances of success for all our efforts and make a significant difference in more than just a handful of communities as we move forward?

I also challenge our leadership. We have many pulls on our limited financial resources. However, in some of our communities our own-source revenues are finally being generated. So I ask: If we expect the other governments to support our postcolonial ambitions, are we dedicating enough of our own resources to kicking down the postcolonial door? There is no better investment a community can make in its future than investing in social change. Sometimes, perhaps unknowingly, I think we simply perpetuate a neocolonial system through adopting policies and directions that do not support self-sufficiency and, therefore, prosperity. We sometimes copy the colonizer.

What I can say with confidence is that communities that have kicked down the postcolonial door are doing better than those who have not. Sure, they have struggles, but they are different struggles, struggles that are fought with the confidence of empowerment and the ability to make decisions and take responsibility for one's own actions.

So let us recognize the significant ground we have made in the last fifty years, let us take the opportunities that lie before us and seek to empower – individual by individual, community by community, Nation by Nation – so that no single person, no single community, and no single Nation is left out or behind.

As our National Chief has stated, "It is OUR time!"

Idle No More and Recapturing
the Spirit and Intent of the Two Row Wampum

Adapted from opening plenary, Aboriginal Financial Officers
Association Conference, "Relationship Building: Discovering Solutions
to Complex Issues," February 13, 2013

Having a conversation about finding solutions to complex issues is timely in light of Idle No More, Chief Theresa Spence, and the testing of the relationships between ourselves as Indigenous Peoples as we confront our evolving relationship with the Crown and the ongoing search for solutions to the so-called "Indian" problem – still the most complex and challenging public policy issue facing Canada today. As Indigenous Peoples, we, of course, have many relationships – both personal and collective; within and between families; between and among our Nations, Tribes, or Bands; within our institutions of government, whether Indian Act or beyond; with domestic governments at all levels (local, provincial, federal); within our political organizations; with corporations (whether large or small); and so on. Our relationships have evolved and changed with the passage of time. We need to understand how and why they have changed if we are going to discover solutions to the complex issues we now face.

During the so-called Age of Discovery, from the fifteenth to the seventeenth century, the European colonizers of the Americas were forced to develop a framework in which to relate to our peoples. Principles of discovery reflected in the doctrine of *terra nullius* had to be modified because we were, in fact, here, and the lands were not, of course, vacant. They argued, therefore, that because our peoples were not Christians and (in the eyes of the newcomers) had inferior social systems, that the lands of the Americas could be settled and acquired without regard for our presence or our occupation of the land. Declaring this so justified (to them) a relationship where the Indigenous Peoples were ultimately subjugated to the will of the colonizer.

In Canada, the relationship with the settler government was somewhat different by the time the British arrived. The Crown, rather than simply dismissing our presence out of hand through theological and other arguments, recognized our existence and required that before its subjects could settle our land, the lands would need to be acquired lawfully from us by an official representative of the Crown. Through this process of treaty making, lands were identified as ours, based upon the historical occupation of our peoples' Traditional Territories, with the balance of the lands continuing to have certain ongoing rights attached to them – the right to hunt, fish, and so on. I am, of course, talking about the process of treaty making as set out in King George III's Royal Proclamation of 1763.

It is the principles of the enduring treaty relationship that to this day continue to underpin how many of our peoples view their current relationship with the Crown, and therefore Canada – where their ancestors entered into relations based upon what they understood to be mutual respect and understanding. In some cases, the symbolic expression of treaty making is reflected in the Wampum Belt. Although not a part of my culture, Wampum is made of white and purple seashells from the Atlantic that are woven into belts. Particular patterns symbolize events, alliances, and people. Wampum was used to form relationships, propose marriage, atone for murder, or even ransom captives. Before Confederation, some of our Nations indicated their assent to treaty by presenting Wampum to officials of the Crown. I understand that the Two Row Wampum Belt of the Iroquois symbolizes an agreement of mutual respect and peace between the Iroquois and European newcomers. The principles embodied in the belt are a set of rules governing the behaviour of the two groups. The Wampum Belt tells us that neither group will force their laws, traditions, customs, or language on each other but will coexist peacefully.

Now fast forward to January 24 last year and the 2012 Crown–First Nations Gathering in Ottawa, during which some First Nations leaders from Ontario presented to Prime Minister Harper a replica Wampum Belt. For these Nations, the expression of that original relationship as understood by their ancestors was, once again, conveyed formally to the Crown.

Fast forward again one more year to January 10, 2013, in the Delta Hotel in Ottawa, when some of those same leaders that presented the Wampum to the Prime Minister the year before stood in front of their Indigenous colleagues – namely, the National Chief, myself, members of the AFN executive, and other Chiefs and leaders – holding a Wampum Belt. At the time, our leadership was debating whether or not to meet with the Prime Minister, a meeting which had been arranged for the next day, January 11, in an effort to satisfy the requests of Chief Spence so she could end her hunger strike. The debate was about whether or not we should go because the governor general would not be attending at the same meeting as the Prime Minister.

As I stood there listening to the impassioned dialogue, the complexity of the relationship challenges we face as Indigenous Peoples sank in. I reflected on our past and on our current moment in time and how, as our relationship with the Crown has evolved, so, too, have our relationships amongst ourselves. I further thought about how our citizens through the use of social media were participating in Idle No More events and how the solutions to our plight have been slow in coming and not broadly implemented. I asked myself, *What can we do today that has not been tried before, and what can we do better?*

And then I reminded myself just how far we have actually come in the recognition of our title and rights, including treaty rights – after all, we have section 35 in the Constitution Act and now the UNDRIP, and we have won over 170 court cases. So today our challenge is not to refight the fights from forty years ago – our challenge today is to actually translate hard-fought rights into practical and meaningful benefits on the ground in our communities to improve the lives of our people and to ensure no community is left out or behind.

To accomplish this vision, each of our citizens and, in turn, each of our Nations, if not already doing so, needs to deal with the colonial legacy of what occurred during the intervening years between when the first Wampum Belt was offered to the Crown and our reality today. Between the time the Wampum Belt was first given to the Crown and then re-presented last year, the original spirit and intent of the treaties has been overshadowed and diminished by the public policy of the federal govern-ment, which was designed to assimilate and remove the "Indian" from his or her culture to become, in the eyes of the settler government, a full and contributing citizen of Canada. Of course, the most insidious of tools used to propagate this policy was the 1876 Indian Act – a law that applied to all Indians who under section 91(24) of Canada's Constitution are the respon-sibility of the federal government. Rather than being citizens or members of a Nation or Tribes of Indians recognized in the treaty relationship as symbolized by the Wampum Belt, under the Indian Act all "Indians" were made wards of the state with the government being our trustee. As Indian Act Indians, we were considered legally incompetent until such time as we enfranchised and became full citizens of Canada, at which point we were no longer recognized as Indigenous and, consequently, lost our political voice within our Nations, lost access to, or ownership of, any lands we shared an interest in on reserve, and so on.

Indian Act government is, accordingly, not self-government and is certainly not an expression of self-determination – it is an impoverished notion of government where the Chief and council are, for the most part, glorified Indian Agents delivering federal programs and services on behalf of Canada, where band councils have limited recognized legal authority to enact laws or make important decisions, and where accountability is pri-marily to Canada and not to our citizens.

So as I stood there listening to my colleagues a few short weeks ago on January 10, I could also not help but to think that with the exception of a few people in the room, all of those leaders, including myself, were some-how a product of that very Indian Act system that we now need to become decolonized from. While I come from a society that has hereditary Chiefs, I am, in fact, an elected councillor of an Indian Act band. The same is true of my friends who stood in front of me holding the Wampum Belt, which symbolically represented the antithesis of what we all represented as Indian Act Chiefs or products of the Indian Act system. This irony was not lost on me.

So why am I telling you this?

In my own province of BC, for the most part our Nations and Tribes have never entered into treaties. But the reality is, whether your Nation or Tribe has a treaty or not, due to Canadian public policy we are all in the same boat, and practically speaking, and even legally, it really makes little difference, as the same policies and same Indian Act has applied to us all, and for the most part still does.

I was also thinking to myself as we debated whether or not to meet with the Prime Minister (with the Wampum Belt clearly in my sights), *How do we actually get back to the original treaty relationship, as represented by that belt, both for those Nations that actually have treaties and for those Nations that do not? How do we rebuild our Nations and re-establish legitimate institutions of government with appropriate jurisdiction and thereby establish healthier relationships, both among ourselves within and between communities as rebuilt Nations and, in turn, with Canada?*

When we met with the Prime Minister on January 11 we did, in fact, talk about this from the perspective of creating new machinery of government in Canada and dealing, once and for all, with implementing the original treaty relationship for those Nations with treaties and to deal with the comprehensive claims process for those Nations that do not have treaties. At some point, ultimately, this work becomes one and the same.

It is in this context that I want to talk briefly about some of the solutions our Nations have found or are working towards in order to decolonize and move beyond the Indian Act and what we are doing to share our stories. But before I do, I want each of you who are First Nations – many of you who live on a reserve, as I do, or come from a band somewhere in Canada – to ask yourself this question: If, tomorrow, there was a vote to be held in your community on whether or not your community should become self-governing and move beyond the Indian Act, would the vote pass or fail and why? And how would you vote?

As Indigenous People living in Canada, we all need to consider these questions, because, ultimately, these are the questions each and every one of our citizens (including you, if your Nation is still under the Indian Act) will have to answer if we are to truly turn Indigenous Rights into political and social change on the ground – to make widespread progress and to move beyond our debilitating colonial past. This is because, as perverse as it may sound, short of a court case declaring all or part of the Indian Act *ultra vires*, it continues to apply until our citizens vote the colonizer out. As wards of the state, the Government of Canada will not release us from their fiduciary grip until they are confident that we actually agree to be released.

Through my office of Regional Chief, I have the privilege to visit many communities and have had this conversation and asked these questions to many of our leaders and to our citizens – and not just to the political leaders but also to Elders, teachers, parents, and so on. And while our people support our political and legal claims to self-determination and us, as leaders, advocating for their rights (in fact, many of them have been carrying placards and going to demonstrations and protests as part of the Idle No More movement to make this very point), they are, nevertheless, often anxious and fearful of change and fearful of self-government.

Disturbingly, it is in this space of fear and uncertainty that the federal government and its bureaucracy looks to enact new laws to govern our people and to create the legal framework for moving beyond the Indian Act by continuing to decide what policies should apply to us and what is in our best interests. This is, of course, not acceptable and will not work. If we are to stop Canada's neocolonial legislative agenda, we have to first understand that we must decolonize ourselves, starting in our communities where we must engage our citizens so that there is enough strength locally to direct and support the change and to implement our rights on the ground. We have no other option – we all have to be Idle No More.

So how do our people move beyond what I call the "fiduciary gridlock" of life under the Indian Act, where there is a dependency on the Crown, to a place where we are self-determining in what I truly believe is the spirit of the Wampum Belts that are held in such high esteem by those Nations that have them? It is not easy to make the transition as a subjugated people living day to day in a colonial reality and to walk through what I like to call the postcolonial door. The colonial legacy is a heavy burden: the poverty, the health and social issues, the breakdown of our institutions of social order, and the general dysfunction, the apathy and unhealthy relationships that still plague many of our communities – basically the crippling legal and economic dependency.

But the good news is that despite this reality for many, we are having success, and we are moving away from dysfunction and dependency through empowerment. We need to build on this success. We need to intensify the level of conversation, share our stories about the solutions that are already well underway, and develop additional solutions and in the process rebuild our Nations, one relationship at a time.

Interestingly, at the January 11 meeting with the Prime Minister, he asked if we had solutions. Indeed, he challenged us that he wanted to hear solutions. And, of course, we gave him some, not all, and certainly not all, worked through, but solutions were discussed and will continue to be discussed and acted upon.

Today, there are now, in fact, over forty former Indian Act bands that are self-governing within Canada and dozens more are involved in some form of governance reform – whether sectoral or comprehensive. In BC, over 70 percent of our Nations are involved in governance reform based on the solutions they have found or are developing.

As previously mentioned, it is troubling that during this transition period, as we move away from governance under the Indian Act and despite the Prime Minister asking for solutions, Canada seems insistent on redesigning our governance for us. I am, of course, talking about the recent government-sponsored legislation dealing with matters such as accountability and transparency [now Bill C-27], safe drinking water, matrimonial real property, and so on. To be clear, any solution that purports to design or impose governance structures on our Nations will ultimately fail if it is not seen as legitimate in the eyes of our people.

As leaders, it is our challenge and responsibility to work to ensure that when our citizens direct change and when our Nations are ready that Canada does not act as gatekeeper to our liberation and restrict opening up that postcolonial door. Canada, the provinces, and Canadians generally must be willing partners and support our individual healing and Nation-rebuilding agenda.

It is, of course, not realistic to expect that each of our small communities (for the most part Indian Act bands) would be able to reinvent themselves and assume jurisdiction over the full range of subject matters that ultimately need to be governed or administered. Nation rebuilding, therefore, is and will continue to occur at a level also beyond the band – typically as an aggregation of bands at the tribal level. In some cases, it may involve Nations opting to use existing institutions and structures of government within Canada – whether federal, provincial, or Aboriginal. In other cases, new institutions will probably need to be established. For example, it is probably not feasible that each community will design curricula, certify teachers, or set standards for education and that some form of broader institutional support is required.

What is important is that as our individual Nations take on governance responsibility and exercise their rights that there is institutional support and, where so desired, the ability to delegate authority to these bodies and aggregate. There are, in fact, in addition to provincial First Nations institutions, now a number of national First Nations institutions providing support to our Nations and in some cases even providing regulatory functions.

It may come as a surprise to some Canadians that we still need a simple legal mechanism in Canada for an Indian Act band to reconstitute itself as a self-governing Nation that is both legitimate in the eyes of its citizens and recognized by other governments. Developing such a mechanism was recommended by the Royal Commission on Aboriginal Peoples and in numerous other reports and studies. There have even been attempts at legislative reforms – either constitutional or otherwise – all failed for a variety of reasons. Finding a practical mechanism to facilitate our exit from the Indian Act is long overdue and an idea whose time has come.

This is why, as one of our proposed solutions, we have, through the BCAFN, developed with our friends in the Senate private member's Bill S-212 [which has since fallen off the order paper], An Act Providing for the Recognition of Self-Governing First Nations of Canada. The bill is currently at second reading in the Senate. Bill S-212 provides that where, at their choice, a First Nation or group of First Nations develops its own Constitution that has been ratified by its citizens, Canada would be required legally to recognize that Nation as self-governing. Following recognition, Canada would then be required to enter into intergovernmental negotiations with respect to that Nation's law-making powers and a new fiscal relationship. Developing S-212 was no small undertaking. However, it cannot be considered to be in its final form, and there is still work needed to improve it and ensure that the bill satisfies the needs of our Nations – there will be a requirement for more concentrated discussion. Bill S-212 should now be studied thoroughly, debated across the country and, as required, amended.

When we developed the bill we were, of course, under no illusion that the government would actually support it. It is not, after all, a government-sponsored initiative. We also expected opposition from some First Nations. For me, because S-212 was drafted taking into consideration our Nations' experiences with self-government, it represents our best collective thinking on the issues at this time and an important step in the right direction. Regardless (and whether or not, as amended, it ultimately becomes law in this or a future Parliament), it stands out today as a legitimate challenge to the federal government's current neocolonial legislative agenda for our peoples that seeks to tinker around the edges of the Indian Act and design our post-Indian Act governance for us.

Ultimately, it is my hope that self-government recognition legislation will support, in a meaningful way, the extraordinary efforts of our First Nations across the country to build strong and appropriate governance and support their efforts to move through the postcolonial door. Moving our Nation-rebuilding agenda forward for all First Nations will take leadership, by both Canada and by our Nations. And we can no longer simply say it is too difficult or too big a task if we are serious about improving the lives of our people. Ask yourself, *What role can I play?* It could be as simple and significant as making a point of informing yourself and your family about the issues and the options for change, to perhaps even taking the lead in being part of that change.

For me, this is what Idle No More really means – not simply a protest movement of disaffected angry young men and women but people who want to build – the true "grass roots," whose voices for far too long have been ignored or overpowered, the voices of yours and my neighbour next door, back home, or perhaps the person who moved away from home because they could not stand the band politics or could not get a job or house, or the woman who was not welcome because she married a non-Native and was no longer considered an Indian Act "Indian" by the government and, consequently, her own people.

On the Parallels, and Differences, between Canada and South Africa

Closing comments, "The Place of Reconciliation,"
Assembly of First Nations Special Chiefs Assembly, December 12, 2013

On the opening day of this Assembly, we all learned that our National Chief was on his way to honour Madiba – representing not only us as the First Peoples of these lands but all Canadians in celebrating the inspiring life of Nelson Mandela and his vision of reconciliation. When great leaders and visionaries pass on – while a time for mourning – it is also a time for self-reflection and contemplation.

The passing of Madiba is an important moment for all of Canada. Former prime ministers are rightfully being stood up for their support in ending apartheid. Yet, at the very same time, our country still struggles with reconciling the pre-existence of our peoples' distinct societies – our Nations – with the assumed sovereignty of the Crown. We struggle with the fact that most of our peoples are not self-governing but rather are governed over – separate and apart from other Canadians under the Indian Act – a legislative instrument that the framers of colonial South Africa consulted when legally constructing apartheid.

There are, of course, obvious parallels between the colonial legacy of South Africa and Canada, as there are differences. Both Canada and South Africa are modern nation-states created through colonial enterprise, with national boundaries dividing tribal territories, artificially penned by European powers. Unlike South Africa, in Canada, as Indigenous Peoples, we are the minority.

Like South Africa, Canada is not the same country as it was when Madiba was jailed in 1962. But while politically, and then legally, apartheid may have ended in South Africa, and while in Canada Aboriginal Title and Rights may be enshrined in the Canadian Constitution and upheld by the courts – the promise of emancipation for Indigenous Peoples in both countries has yet to be fully realized. Many still suffer under the vestiges of colonialism. Legal rights have not been transformed into economic and social change. Justice has not been realized.

In South Africa, issues with governance, low education outcomes, lack of skilled workers, and unemployment levels at around 40 percent mean the Indigenous population is still economically and socially marginalized and living in Third World poverty. However, do they have the legal and political power – the tools – to do something about it? Yes. Will they? Yes. This is what political and legal freedom demands and the hope of a nation symbolized by that huge smile of Mandela. And it is this spirit of hope through reconciliation that we need to embrace more fully here in Canada, recognizing, as in South Africa, that it is not easy to transition from a colonial reality and the legacy of dysfunction it leaves in its wake.

In Canada, we have begun the process of reconciliation, but unlike in South Africa we do not have all the tools to take back control of our lives and our destiny. In modern times, our peoples' path to reconciliation arguably started soon after the 1969 White Paper and our reaction to attempts at assimilation. By 1982, we had fought for section 35 with additional attempts at constitutional reform. The path to reconciliation was further laid with the Prime Minister's apology in 2008 – followed soon thereafter by the creation of our own Truth and Reconciliation Commission, looking into the dark history of the residential schools.

However, as a country, we still have a long way to go to both heal but also to advance and change the legal framework under which our peoples – our Nations – coexist within a Canada where all peoples can see their reflection when looking into the mirror of the Constitution. The work of reconciliation must be accelerated.

There is a growing lack of trust among our peoples with other governments, particularly in light of proposed resource development and proposed federal legislation dealing with the education of our children. To help build trust, Canada, for its part, needs to commit to developing a broad reconciliation framework to guide all departments and ministries and facilitate meaningful engagement with our Nations. Today, such a framework does not exist in this country, and there are limited or no mechanisms to actually reconcile even if, politically, there is the will to do so. The concepts of our peoples making "claims" and negotiating final agreements – the premise of which is fundamentally flawed – need to give way to engagement based on principles of recognition and reconciliation. This is not about scattered programs or initiatives – it is a national project that requires the full engagement and the commitment of the highest level of government. Beyond the apology offered in 2008, beyond the important work of truth telling and of healing, reconciliation requires laws to change and policies to be rewritten. It requires our legitimate political institutions to be recognized and empowered and the laws they make enforceable.

And I know that there are some of you that do not trust (or have no faith) that under this (or any) government reconciliation will ever occur. We all understand, appreciate, and share in your concerns. But let me also say this: mistrust and fear, if based on hate or an inability to forgive, will, as it does everywhere, only perpetuate even more hate and fear, creating hopelessness in our people and prolonging the misery of colonialism.

I know that as we move forward with our own reconciliation efforts back home in each of our Nations, in our conversations between and among ourselves and with others, that there will be things said and things done that frustrate relationships, that frustrate efforts to reconcile. Let's not let these get in the way of the more noble objectives to which, as leaders, we all aspire. When we are truly committed to the principles of reconciliation, then we need not apologize for our fears and the things said and done out of fear but rather move beyond our fears. I know in my heart that the voices and actions of those that openly speak out against reconciliation – whether our voices or those of other Canadians – will fade away into the obscurity of history, replaced by the realized vision of an improved quality of life for our peoples with thriving and practising cultures in a stronger Canada.

At this Assembly, this is what we have been talking about when we speak of Nation building, when we talk about rebuilding our Nations, about building our governments, about the education of our children, about justice and policing and economic opportunities. We do this through implementing the treaties based upon their spirit and intent and also to address our rights in those parts of the country where there are no treaties and unextinguished Aboriginal Title.

To be honest, whether you have a treaty or not, all our Nations are in the same boat of decolonization – of rebuilding and reconciling. We all struggle in talking about getting rid of the Indian Act – an apartheid-era instrument that, ironically, our citizens often have trouble letting go of and which still determines the makeup of this very Assembly.

So, we all need to ask ourselves: Are we ready for reconciliation? Government of Canada, are you ready? Are Canadians ready? Is your Nation ready? Are your citizens ready? How will you govern your lands? How will decision-making power be shared, both between our governments and with other governments?

As former National Chief Ovide Mercredi so eloquently laid out on the first day of our Assembly, this is the work we all need to do and the work that the Chiefs in northern Manitoba are undertaking in re-establishing their institutions of governance, based on their treaties, to aspire to more than being "bands" under the Indian Act and to overcome the impoverished notion of governance where we are Indian Agents delivering programs and services on behalf of Canada. Each of our Nations has to do this work – hard and often unforgiving work but, all the same, work necessary as a prerequisite to full reconciliation with the Crown. It is also the foundational work from which we can all combine our strength as true Nations moving forward in assemblies such as this.

There is a reason why the National Chief was asked to perform the ceremony he did in leading the Canadian delegation and causing an eagle feather to be laid to rest with Madiba. Madiba may have been the head of a once colonial and now modern nation-state – South Africa – but Madiba and his peoples are from Tribal Nations, as we all are. They have hereditary systems like our Tribes. But while tribalism may be a fact, as Indigenous Peoples we will never realize our individual aspirations as Nations unless we set aside our tribalism in favour of working together. At some point, we need to have a broader conversation about aggregation and creating more effective machinery of government – not just at our Nation level but beyond. *To be sure, no sovereignty in today's world is absolute, including ours.* Nations need to partner – we need to partner – amongst ourselves and beyond. No person, no community, no Nation, indeed no state, is an island. We all breathe the same air and drink the same water.

Political freedoms and legal rights are not the answer alone. Rights and freedoms must be acted upon. Emancipation takes the courage of the emancipated to actually rebuild, to work even harder, and to realize new opportunities in the face of ongoing challenges and hurdles.

By working together, we demonstrate to our citizens and to all Canadians that First Nations are not only up for this challenge but that, collectively, we will achieve the change that is needed and true reconciliation. We are inspired by the legacy of Madiba and in our own humble way aspire to make his vision a reality right here in Canada – for all peoples across this country.

Our Shared Histories
and the Path of Reconciliation

Adapted from Australian National University Annual
Reconciliation Lecture, November 9, 2016

Both here, in Australia, and in Canada we are pursuing a path of reconciliation. Our countries have much in common. Both former British colonies,
we are the product of colonialism, with all of the resulting losses and harms
to Indigenous Lands, legal and governing systems, languages, cultures, and
even lives. Our countries are both still coming to terms with our colonial
pasts and rooting out colonial attitudes that undermine the modern relationships between the descendants of First Peoples and the newcomers. It takes
courage and hard work, but our postcolonial countries are stronger and
more successful for embracing reconciliation. Our Prime Minister, Justin
Trudeau, has said publicly that "there is no relationship more important to
me and to Canada than the one with Indigenous Peoples." He has tasked all
of his ministers to work towards rebuilding a nation-to-nation relationship
based on the recognition of rights, respect, cooperation, and partnership.

In Canada, there is a sometimes little understood transformation occurring as Indigenous Nations rebuild and move through what I like to call the
postcolonial door, re-establishing their institutions of good governance
and taking their rightful place within our Confederation. I would like to
provide some historical, legal, and political context to this transformation
and speak about what our government is doing in support of the important

work of reconciliation and Nation rebuilding – critical not only to the future of Indigenous Peoples but the future of our great country.

For many years, I and many other leaders have worked for change – or to change the laws and policies of Canada's federal government, including the Indian Act, which dates back to 1876. I have always regarded the Indian Act as an enormous impediment on the road to reconciliation, the antithesis of self-government as an expression of self-determination. It was a point of view that I advocated for as Regional Chief representing British Columbia at the Assembly of First Nations, an organization in our country representing more than 630 First Nations communities, nearly 1 million people across Canada.

Given my past experience, you might wonder or ask why I would decide to run to be a Member of Parliament for Canada. And to be honest, taking the leap into federal politics was not easy for me, nor was the decision taken lightly. I cannot claim to have wanted or had a long-standing desire to be a Member of Parliament, let alone a minister of the Crown. However, during my time as Regional Chief for British Columbia, I came to a greater appreciation that Indigenous Peoples could not get the work done without willing federal and provincial partners. I also realized that new approaches to reconciliation were required.

And then, about this time, I met a guy named Justin Trudeau. I met him for the first time about three and a half years ago when he came up to see me in the Yukon. We were in the Yukon for an annual general assembly for the Assembly of First Nations, and he attended one of our working sessions, a working session that I happened to be chairing and where we were dealing with questions of Nation rebuilding and of reconciliation. Afterwards, we sat down and chatted. We talked about the future of Canada, about making Canada even better, and in particular we talked about his convictions with respect to Indigenous Peoples. We talked about what we shared in common, including talking about walking in the footsteps of our political fathers, who actually knew each other. His father, of course, was more well known than mine. But our then soon-to-be Prime Minister eventually asked me if I would consider running as part of his team in the 2015 federal election.

I did not agree right away, if you can imagine, but eventually came to see my candidacy as a chance to be part of a government whose leader has made a solemn commitment to fundamental change with a vision for true reconciliation with Indigenous Peoples as a function of an inclusive, just, and respectful society. And now, having been appointed Minister of Justice and Attorney General of Canada, essentially the steward of the Canadian justice system, I am responsible for the very laws and policies that so many of us had worked so hard to change.

Even though it has just been a year and about four or five days since the appointment, I still sometimes have to sit back and reflect, and it still takes a moment to sink in, and I see my appointment not so much as a personal accomplishment but rather as a symbol of what the appointment represents and how far we have come as a country. Not so long ago, an Indigenous woman like me would not have been allowed to vote, let alone run for office or practise as a lawyer. Today, an Indigenous woman is the chief law officer of the Crown, and I hope and take on this tremendous responsibility with absolute vigour. That symbolism became even more potent when you consider the history of Indigenous Peoples.

When the Fathers of Canadian Confederation came together in 1867 to lay the foundation for Canada, Indigenous Peoples were not present. They were left out. This despite the early treaty making and the many political and military alliances made with Indigenous Peoples, including those under the auspices of the Royal Proclamation of 1763. During the time of the Proclamation, the colonial authorities recognized the power of various Nations or Tribes of Indians and the need to make treaties. The fact that Indigenous Peoples were left out of Confederation in 1867 as partners has had far-reaching implications for Canada in the tumultuous intervening years. And in many ways, what we're doing today is correcting that mistake.

Before Confederation, some of the Tribes in eastern Canada indicated their assent to treaty by presenting Wampum to officials of the Crown. The Wampum Belt – shells on leather – reflects an understanding that neither group will force their laws, traditions, customs, or language on the other but will coexist peacefully through mutual recognition. The laws of the Tribe, in their canoe in the river, are symbolized by one row of purple shells, and those of the newcomers, in their boat, are also symbolized by a row of purple shells. While the two rivers exist side by side, they will never cross.

Unfortunately, after Confederation, Crown policy became one of assimilation, not partnership. While historical treaty making did continue up to the 1930s, for the governments of the day, the treaties were seen as little more than land surrenders. The legislative tool used to propagate the policy of assimilation – regardless of whether or not the Tribe had a treaty – was the Indian Act, a law that applied to all "Indians" who, under Canada's Constitution, are the legal responsibility of the federal government. Rather than being citizens or members of a Nation or Tribes of Indians, recognized in the treaty relationship and symbolized by the Wampum Belt, under the Indian Act, legally defined Indians were moved onto reserves, made wards of the state with the government being their trustee.

The Indian Act system of administration partitioned the precontact Indigenous Nations, the 60-plus Nations – or "peoples," as the term is used and understood in the United Nations Declaration on the Rights of Indigenous Peoples – into 630-plus administrative Indian Act bands living in some 1,000-plus reserve communities. Indian Act Indians were considered legally incompetent until such time as they enfranchised, becoming full citizens of Canada, at which point they were no longer recognized as Indigenous and consequently lost their political voice within their Nation, lost access to or ownership of any lands they shared an interest in on reserves, and so on.

Similar to Australia, the Indian Act also created residential schools whose sole purpose was to take the Indian out of the child. Those schools told children every day that their culture – the culture of their ancestors – was inferior. Children were forbidden from speaking their languages and following their cultural practices. Worse, many of them suffered unimaginable abuse in the schools. Some children never came home. The traumatizing effects of these events have echoed through Indigenous communities over the years. Women and girls in particular were left vulnerable through cycles of violence and abuse that carried through generations. Ironically, even though the policy objective of the Indian Act was to assimilate Indigenous Peoples, it also discouraged them from participating in Canadian society.

I believe it is not an overexaggeration to say that it is one of the most insidious tools ever used to subjugate peoples.

Thankfully, our world has changed and continues to change. The signs of change point towards a recognition that Indigenous Peoples are distinct groups within their respective countries with special rights that need to be protected and acted upon. In the modern era, the approach that Canada chose was to expressly recognize and affirm Indigenous Peoples and their Aboriginal and Treaty Rights when our Constitution was patriated from the United Kingdom in 1982.

In Canada, our modern legal system is underpinned by the recognition of fundamental human rights. The Constitution Act of 1982 includes a Charter of Rights and Freedoms as well as specific provisions dealing with Aboriginal Rights. In many ways, my role as Minister of Justice and Attorney General of Canada can be seen as somewhat of an ambassador for the Charter and to ensure that all laws and policies of the state uphold the Charter of Rights and Freedoms.

Today, Aboriginal Rights are an important part of our legal framework and shape how the Crown and Indigenous Peoples manage their relationship moving forward. Including these rights in our Constitution amounted to a promise to Indigenous Peoples that their presence in Canada and their rights would no longer be denied, that assimilation and marginalization were colonial relics of the past, and that Canadians were ready to work together with them to build a better Canada. Meeting this promise has not come easily, and change did not and has not happened overnight, and there's still much work to be done.

Interestingly, Aboriginal Rights were not originally going to be included in the Constitution. However, in the face of considerable legal and political pressure, they eventually were. In fact, at the time of patriation, some legal advisers to the provinces played down the significance of section 35, advising their clients that any continuing Aboriginal Rights were limited and that they did not need to worry about the implications of the constitutional provisions. For these folks, section 35 was a so-called empty box that could only be populated at the will of the Crown. In other words, there really were no inherent rights, including the right of self-government, the constitutional division of powers having been fully exhausted between the federal government and the provincial governments.

At the time of patriation, some Indigenous leaders were not comfortable with section 35, fearing the domestication of rights or that perhaps the empty boxers were right. However, the vast majority of Indigenous leaders in our country supported section 35, and for those that had fought so vigorously for it and for the Charter amendments – including my father – it was, of course, anything but an empty box.

One of the provisions of the new Constitution called for a series of constitutional conferences in the early 1980s to set out the scope and the extent of the rights recognized in section 35 and, in particular, the right of self-government. During the constitutional conferences that ensued, the disconnect between the Indigenous views and the government's views was palpable at the negotiating table.

I remember in 1983, as a young girl, watching the conference at school. I was in Grade 6, and my father and our current Prime Minister's father – then Prime Minister Pierre Elliott Trudeau – I watched them go toe to toe. When the negotiations were going nowhere, my father, in his inimitable way, told Trudeau Senior that "there needs to be some good faith about it and that the exercise now is not about frank and open discussion or understanding an appreciation of the other people's concerns on the basis of respect and dignity. It has now become all of a sudden a question of power and who exercises it."

René Lévesque, then premier of Quebec, summed it up best when he said later that day: "Behind all of this, what is going on is a political process, a political process that is fundamentally a question of power. One authorized spokesperson of the Aboriginal Peoples has already stated the whole thing is about power." Premier Lévesque continued to say: "Power has traditionally been exercised in several classic ways. Probably the most classic example is by force of arms and by the strength of numbers. For example, the dispossession of the Métis during the time of Riel was a crime, which was an abuse of the force of arms backed up by strength of numbers. What alternative is left so a group can realize a civilized solution? It means accumulating enough power, enough ways of asserting pressure, so they can negotiate as equals. That is fundamental." And, of course, he was right. Since the failure of those conferences in the 1980s, Indigenous Peoples in Canada have been doing just that, accumulating enough power – economic, legal, and political power – to reach what Premier Lévesque stated is a civilized solution.

Today, I think we call this reconciliation – reconciling the power of Indigenous Peoples with that of the Crown. And since 1982, our courts have confirmed Indigenous Peoples do have the inherent right of self-government and that these powers survived Confederation. To quote the court, these powers are "one of the unwritten, underlying values of the Constitution outside the distribution to Parliament and the legislatures in 1867." They are not absolute, but they are indeed very real. Reconciliation is now possible precisely because section 35 is not an empty box. The negotiation table has been levelled. Today, it is about sharing power, and it is about cooperative federalism.

With respect to land rights in those parts of the country where no treaties were entered into, either historic or modern, we also have seen clarity provided by our highest court. In 2014, the *Tsilhqot'in* decision, a decision of the Supreme Court of Canada, granted the first declaration of Aboriginal Title to the Tŝilhqot'in Nation in British Columbia. Most commentators, and rightly so, point to the decision as being game changing.

In my view, there were two important elements, or takeaways, of that decision. The first is that in granting the declaration of Aboriginal Title, the court found that title is territorial in nature and not limited to intensively used sites or small spots (which the Crown had previously argued), assuming that there was title in the first place. The second being that title is held collectively by the Nation, the Aboriginal Peoples sharing common language, culture, and history and not the federally imposed Indian Act bands. Both of these findings have critical repercussions for reconciliation moving forward and the need to support Nation rebuilding.

However, it is one thing to have rights on paper or declared by a court and quite another to be able to realize them in practice. The journey of decolonization and reconciliation is complicated, often painful, and certainly never easy. It is not easy to make the transition as a subjugated people living day to day in a colonial reality and to walk through the postcolonial door. There is considerable rebuilding needed. It requires recognition. It requires healing. It requires forgiveness, and it requires trust.

As an important step, in 2008, the Government of Canada apologized to Indigenous Peoples for residential schools. The government also established a reconciliation commission – a truth and reconciliation commission to examine the dark period of our history of residential schools. It was inspired by the commission created in South Africa post-apartheid. The commission documented the stories of abuse told by survivors, while honouring their truths, and it made numerous recommendations – calls to action – in a report it released at the end of 2015 that addressed aspects of the reconciliation project through the lens of residential school survivors and experience. Our government has committed to implementing the calls to action through improving education, child welfare, health care in Indigenous communities, and protecting the languages and culture of Indigenous Peoples.

Our government has also taken another important step towards reconciliation and facing another dark legacy: the over 1,200 Indigenous women and girls who have gone murdered or reported missing by the RCMP – and I know the numbers are higher than that. Although Indigenous women make up 4 percent of Canada's female population, 16 percent of all women murdered in Canada between 1980 and 2012 were Indigenous. This past August, the Government of Canada launched an independent National Inquiry into Missing and Murdered Indigenous Women and Girls. And there is no question that the combined work of the Truth and Reconciliation Commission and now the Inquiry into Murdered and Missing Indigenous Women and Girls will be invaluable in the healing journey of reconciliation and in deconstructing our colonial legacy.

But as the late, great Nelson Mandela taught us, beyond the necessary apologies and beyond the emotional work of truth telling and healing, reconciliation actually requires laws to change and policies to be rewritten. And it is in this regard that I see my role as Minister of Justice – as ensuring our country's laws and policies actually do change based on the recognition of rights. And there are numerous policies and laws that need to change and new ones developed. Political and legal reconciliation in furtherance of the nation-to-nation relationship is a national project that requires significant coordination and commitment at the highest level of government.

So, you may ask, Where do we start? What is needed to be done to rebuild Indigenous Nations, to actually get back to the original relationship as represented by the Wampum Belt, both for those nations that have treaties and for those that do not? The good news is that over the last thirty years since Aboriginal and Treaty Rights were recognized in our Constitution, as Aboriginal Title and Rights have crystallized in the courts, many Indigenous Nations in Canada have already begun rebuilding and have demonstrated success, often with little fanfare and little media attention, developing their own institutions of governance – some at the local level, others regional, and sometimes Canada-wide in scope, some as a result of modern treaty making, others as part of sectoral governance initiatives. There is much that can be learned from this work, and we need to build on that success.

In Canada, we have something called a Community Well-Being Index, and the evidence is clear. Self-governing communities are doing significantly better, both socially and economically, than those that are not. Today, there are over forty former Indian Act bands that are recognized as self-governing within Canada, and dozens more are involved in some form of governance reform, whether sectoral or comprehensive. In fact, approximately one-third of our Nations are involved in some form of governance reform based on the solutions that they have found and are developing, working in cooperation with the Crown.

For example, in the area of land management, communities are developing land codes that replace those sections in the Indian Act with their own laws dealing with on-reserve land management, including the creation of interests in land, how they are transferred, and land-use decisions made. There are regional initiatives where communities can make laws with respect to health and health care delivery and education. About a third of communities are developing or have developed financial administration laws. Others are collecting property or goods-and-services taxes. A group of communities is collectively issuing debentures and raising monies on the bond market secured by their own-source revenues to build much-needed infrastructure.

However, while progress has been made, the pace of change is far too slow and not evenly spread across the country. In most cases, the foundational work of Nation rebuilding through re-establishing core institutions of governance beyond the Indian Act has not occurred. There is, in truth, no simple legal mechanism for recognition in Canada that supports the transition away from the colonial-imposed systems when a Nation is ready, willing, and able to resume control. There have been many attempts at recognition legislation in the past, but they have gone nowhere.

By some accounts, at the current pace – using existing mechanisms for legal and political reconciliation to support Nation rebuilding – it would take generations for all Nations to move through the postcolonial door. This is obviously not acceptable and clearly demands a need for a more concerted effort by government with new legislative tools and other mechanisms to support Nation rebuilding – something that our government has committed to doing, working in partnership with Indigenous Peoples.

At the highest level, the United Nations Declaration provides a framework for reconciliation, setting minimum standards, and is instructive on how we develop our own made-in-Canada framework for reconciliation, reflecting our history and our unique and strong legal and constitutional framework. Above all else, this framework for reconciliation must be grounded in a commitment to principles. Those principles should not only be grounded in law but should also demonstrate a commitment to go beyond existing legal obligations to strengthen the nation-to-nation relationship. A commitment to a renewed nation-to-nation relationship between the government and Indigenous Peoples should be based on the recognition and implementation of the inherent rights of Indigenous Peoples. It should acknowledge the centrality of the honour of the Crown in all processes, and it should understand that treaties and agreements and other constructive arrangements between the Crown and Indigenous Peoples are acts of reconciliation based on mutual recognition and respect, and that mechanisms for reconciliation must be developed in partnership with Indigenous Peoples.

Re-establishing the nation-to-nation relationship, practically speaking, means deconstructing the Indian Act system, where it still applies, and getting rid of imposed administrative structures and replacing them with self-governing Nations. This is the work that excites me the most because, as an Indigenous Canadian, I know it is essential to ensuring practising and thriving cultures.

So, additionally, as Minister of Justice, there are other ways my department is supporting reconciliation. For example, we are reviewing our litigation strategy to ensure that the positions we take in court are in line with our commitments to a renewed nation-to-nation relationship that is based on recognition of rights. Also, as part of my broader mandate – big mandate – from the Prime Minister, we have initiated a full review of our justice system. Just as the Inquiry into Murdered and Missing Indigenous Women and Girls examines how Indigenous women have been victimized, our government has committed to tackling the overrepresentation of Indigenous Peoples, both as victims and offenders, in the criminal justice system – another symptom of marginalization, poverty, and the legacy of colonization. Our review of the justice system is focusing on problems that make the system less efficient and less fair, which can reduce access to justice. Working across government, this review is looking at how measures such as restorative justice and sentencing circles can provide off-ramps to the justice system and possibly lead to lower incarceration rates for non-violent offences. Sentencing circles, as an Indigenous legal tradition, are something that all Canadians can learn and benefit from. In my opinion, the nation-to-nation relationship and the resurgence of Aboriginal governance based on Indigenous legal traditions will, over the next generation, change for the better the way Canada is governed, not only in transforming Indigenous Nations but transforming our country as a whole.

Rights and Recognition

"

Political freedoms and legal rights
are not the answer alone.
Rights and freedoms must be acted upon.

"

Fiduciary Gridlock and
the Inherent Right of Self-Government

Adapted from an address to "2013 State of the Federation:
Aboriginal Multilevel Governance," Institute of Intergovernmental
Relations, Queen's University, November 28, 2013

The resurgence of Aboriginal governance, based on Indigenous laws and Indigenous legal traditions, will, over the next generation, change the way Canada is governed – not only in transforming Indigenous Nations but our country, for I believe that truly having a third order of government in Canada with real powers and real influence will be good for the federation and for creating the proper national balance. As Aboriginal Peoples take back control of our lives, so, too, will all Canadians take back control, ensuring we have a Canada that I think we all aspire to live in, a country based on shared values and principles that we have spent years as a nation fostering – creating a caring and liberal society that until very recently ensured our place on this planet as a favoured nation and one of the best countries in which to live. So, from an Aboriginal perspective, I want to focus on our solutions and the opportunities we have for strengthening the federation, where, in the spirit of partnership, we look to complete the project of federalism and where the promise of federalism is enjoyed by both Aboriginal and non-Aboriginal Canadians alike.

Before Confederation, some of our Nations indicated their assent to treaty by presenting Wampum to officials of the Crown. The Wampum Belt stipulates that neither group will force their laws, traditions, customs, or language on each other but will coexist peacefully. Considerable water has flowed down the symbolic river of the Two Row Wampum Belt since it was originally presented. And while we need to get back to the spirit and intent of the Two Row Wampum, the nature of the relationship in a modern nation-state has changed. The laws of our respective peoples are not simply in their own boat or canoe, side by side. As the common law has evolved, with new legal principles being developed, and notwithstanding the 1867 constitutional division of powers, the reality today is a Canada with multi-level governance, where the federal, provincial, territorial, and our re-emerging Aboriginal governments share power and decision making between and among each other, where existing and evolving legal principles such as cooperative federalism increasingly guide the complex web of authority for governments to make laws, often in the same area, and to actually govern effectively.

Since 1867, a lot has happened "constitutionally" with respect to the recognition of our title and rights, including treaty rights. The 1982 patriation of our Constitution and the inclusion of section 35, was, of course, incredibly significant. Thirty years on – and dozens of court cases later – it is our legal reality in Canada that Aboriginal Peoples do have the inherent right of self-government and that these rights survived as, to quote the court, "one of the unwritten 'underlined values' of the Constitution outside the powers distributed to Parliament and the legislatures in 1867." They are not absolute rights, but they are still very real.

So today the question is not, legally, whether there is a right of self-government but rather the question is political: How does pluralism, as a result of these rights, work? What makes this work challenging, and despite the case law, is that there are still deeply divergent perspectives within Canada on what the inherent right means or does not mean that distract us from the difficult political work of reconciliation and the related but fundamental community development work required of each of us in our communities.

There are three clear and conflicting perspectives on the inherent right. The first, advanced by what I will respectfully call First Nations fundamentalists, is that the inherent right provides the basis for First Nations to stand alone from Canada. That is, self-government is a right of sovereignty that at its full expression could result in independence from Canada. Perhaps this perspective is as much a response to the terrible experiences of our people within Confederation at the hands of the colonial governments as it is a true cry for independence. Nevertheless, it is real, reactionary, and aggressive – an approach that has led, and could lead, to more conflict.

The second, juxtaposed to the first, is that the inherent right does not exist at all. This perspective comes from non-Aboriginals who seek to deny Aboriginal Rights and promote a greater role for assimilation of Indigenous Peoples into the institutions and structures of non-Indigenous systems of government and society within Canada. This approach has also led to conflict and helps fuel the fire of those who share the first perspective.

The third perspective, the one that I support and would like to believe the vast majority of all Canadians support, is that the inherent right exists within Canada – within Confederation – and, in doing so, reflects what is unique and special about the idea of Canada: that there is room in our country for different legal traditions and compromise, that our country is one where there is a full box of section 35 rights and our job as a nation is to allow those rights to find their expression through a process of reconciliation. Since patriation in 1982, the work of attempting to bring Aboriginal Peoples more fully into Canada as partners was most public during the constitutional conferences on self-government held during the mid-1980s and then in the work to amend the Constitution in 1992 through the Charlottetown Accord. Certainly, with respect to Aboriginal issues, Charlottetown was, in my opinion, a missed opportunity. The power of self-government and the route to get there would have been more clearly articulated.

I do not know when our country will next look to amend our Constitution. What I know is that when we do open that door, we need to revisit Charlottetown with respect to our peoples' rights. Until then, we need to support existing efforts and develop additional mechanisms to facilitate our peoples' implementing their inherent right and transitioning away from the Indian Act.

In the wake of the Idle No More protests (which is a cry for us all to do better, First Nations and non-First Nations leaders alike), on January 11,

some of us met with Prime Minister Harper, to the sounds of drums outside his office. At the meeting, while not making too many commitments,
Mr. Harper did at least agree that he needed to establish a high-level mechanism to oversee both the reform of the way Canada negotiates modern
treaties and also implements existing ones. Accordingly, Senior Oversight
Committees that include representatives from the Prime Minister's Office,
the Privy Council Office, Aboriginal Affairs and Northern Development
Canada, and the Assembly of First Nations were established. The Prime
Minister also agreed that we needed to get rid of the Indian Act, and he
wanted solutions. We, of course, told him we have solutions.

But the fact is there is still no practical and efficient mechanism in Canada to facilitate a First Nation, or group of First Nations, transitioning
beyond the Indian Act when they are ready, willing, and able to do so. I
know some have challenged us (particularly government officials) that
many First Nations do not appear, when pushed, to want to move out from
under the Indian Act. To which I would say this: they do. However, it is
the policy of the Crown with respect to the transition that is the problem
in areas such as land tenure, taxation, and the application of laws. Still,
while this is an interesting conversation we will continue to have, if a First
Nation or a group of First Nations want to comprehensively remove itself
from the clutches of the Indian Act, today they really only have three
choices: go to court, negotiate, or simply act.

With respect to the practicality of the first choice, although the courts
have said the inherent right to self-government exists, for many reasons it
is not possible for all of our Nations to go to court and test whether they
have jurisdiction over a particular subject matter. With respect to the second,
at the rate self-government negotiations are going, it would take over one
hundred plus years by some accounts for all First Nations to have rudiment-
ary governance beyond the Indian Act in place.

Which leaves the third choice: the direction in which many Nations
are heading because they want to have order in their community, but where
the Nation takes its chances – politically, legally, and financially – of being
challenged. This is obviously not a good situation, because every First Nation needs to have the certainty of legitimate and appropriate governance
to take its rightful place within federation. So creating a more efficient

mechanism for the transition to self-government is a must and has been recommended in numerous reports, commissions, and studies. With the support of the Chiefs in BC, I have made creating this mechanism my political priority as Regional Chief.

In the last Parliament, with the help of our friends in the Senate, we in fact drafted self-government recognition legislation that was introduced as a private member's bill. Our bill, without government support, fell off the order paper. We intend to introduce a new bill this Parliament. Our Self-Government Recognition Act (Bill S-212) would provide that, at their option, individual bands, either individually or in groups, could develop their own self-government proposal, including the Nation's constitution and, once ratified by their citizens, would require Canada to recognize that Nation's post-Indian Act government. No interminable negotiations.

The powers of a "recognized First Nation" would be similar to the powers of the current self-governing First Nations, where the law-making powers or jurisdictions could be drawn down by the Nation over time. The legislation would also establish a new fiscal relationship between the recognized First Nation and the Crown – this would include taxation. And, I should add, our people are not averse to paying tax: what we are averse to is paying tax to the wrong government or one that is not accountable or legitimate in the eyes of our citizens.

While we continue to develop and advance our own solutions, what is very troubling to us, during this transition period, is that Canada continues to redesign our governance for us with its own legislative agenda. While we can all appreciate that some First Nations leaders may want some of this legislation, the legislation is not, for the most part, permissive, and it is being imposed. This is regressive, dangerous, and not consistent with the direction our county has been moving, politically and legally, since 1982.

The names of the government bills – the Family Homes on Reserves and Matrimonial Interests or Rights Act; An Act Respecting the Safety of Drinking Water on First Nation Lands; An Act to Enhance Financial Accountability and Transparency of First Nations – may sound reasonable but on closer examination are simply more examples of Canada telling us how we ought to live. While to the public these may all sound like good initiatives, they do not account for the nature of the relationship and assume that the Crown can still legislate over us at will. I have confrontationally called this "neocolonial" when meeting both publicly and privately with the Prime Minister and am deeply afraid that the government by its actions is only fuelling the fire of those Aboriginal leaders that have a more radical agenda. More importantly, these bills also deny our governments the ability to determine our own policy with respect to our peoples' future.

In some respects, however, I can also appreciate the government's dilemma. The tragedy of "wardship" is that in the absence of emancipation, the colonial authority is legally bound to act in what it believes is in the best interest of its subjects. This clouds the debate on implementing Aboriginal and Treaty Rights and building strong and appropriate First Nations governments. It clouds our work back home in our communities to actually develop the political support to let go of the Indian Act. This is what I call "fiduciary gridlock."

Nevertheless, I am confident that we are well on our way to broader governance reform within our Nations. Self-government recognition legislation would, I know, focus the energy on community development work back home so our people can undertake the hard work of building community trust and consensus and rebuilding governance, where the citizens themselves are empowered to work through their own issues, find the solutions, and take responsibility for implementing them, to aggregate and to deal where necessary with issues such as shared territory and resource development as required.

The need to complete this work will become even more pressing when the first Aboriginal Title declaration is granted by the courts. The *Tsilhqot'in* case, also called *William* in reference to Chief Roger William, the humble and unassuming leader of the Xeni Gwet'in, part of the Tŝilhqot'in Nation, is the latest in the long line of BC Aboriginal Title and Rights cases. While being careful not to prejudge the judgment, I can say this: to those of us in the court, it seemed from their tough questioning of the Crown's lawyers that the justices had come to the conclusion that the trial judge had properly applied their test for proving title. For me, what was most telling was that the bench, having apparently made up their mind on the larger track of the proven title area, was moving on to the next big question: What laws will apply to the title lands so proven? The answer is, of course, multilevel governance. It will be a combination of laws in accordance with the constitutional division of powers and the rules of federalism, as they are evolving. It will be a combination of Tŝilhqot'in law, provincial law, and federal law, and the relationship between laws will have to be addressed through reconciliation discussions among the parties.

So perhaps the first title declaration will be the impetus for true reconciliation – let us hope so. Through the Senior Oversight Committee, we are pushing the federal government to develop a new horizontal federal reconciliation framework to guide all federal departments, negotiators, and other officials tasked with reconciling with our Nations. Such a reconciliation framework would ensure coordination of federal policy in support of a number of reconciliation options – not just modern treaty making.

Our aim is to have Canada eventually get rid of its outdated comprehensive claims policy altogether, the premise of which is fundamentally flawed, and to move away from the idea of so-called final agreements. We are not making claims; we are reconciling, and the process of reconciliation is ongoing, not final. Reconciling with Aboriginal Peoples will, I predict, help change the way we approach government in Canada generally. We often, sometimes glibly, remark that Aboriginal government is a unique form of government – but it truly is. When you consider those Nations that are self-governing today, they typically have powers that are municipal, provincial, and federal – and some that are distinctly Indigenous. It is a hybrid government. No other form of government within Canada has this range of multilevel powers – a blend of section 91 and 92 of the Constitution Act, forged and enhanced on the strength of section 35. We are already seeing the impact of this in BC with the Nisga'a and at Westbank and Tsawwassen and looking to the north in the Yukon.

And speaking of the North, not only is the law-making power unique, so, too, is the geographical distribution of that power. Historically, political power in Canada has rested in the south, where most people live and therefore vote. In this political model, rural Canada is akin to a colony of urban Canada – urban centres exploiting the vast resource wealth. Local communities with their limited governance in rural Canada have little influence over significant public policy decisions that affect them and do not keep much of the wealth generated from resource development. Most of the wealth heads south or farther afield – both in terms of taxes generated and business profits – which, in the case of business profits, are increasingly heading overseas to those who own the companies that operate within our borders.

However, this is changing with re-emerging Aboriginal government, where there is real political power and real control by Aboriginal governments in their Traditional Territories, wherever located. Typically, people who are attached to, live on, and survive off the land they live on take a different perspective to land management and resource exploitation than those who do not or are just passing through. This emerging political reality is already changing the way land-use planning and decision making are being conducted in my province, and as a consequence, more control and more of the wealth is staying in rural BC – much of it controlled by First Nations governments and their business offshoots.

In closing, let me say this. Regardless of whether I am right or wrong about my last two points, for me there is no question that Canada as a whole will be a better place when our peoples are full partners within the federation, and where our distinct and rich cultures continue with an improved quality of life for our peoples with practising and thriving cultures. It is our collective task and responsibility to promote this day. As has been said numerous times before, "We are all here to stay."

Translating Hard-Fought-For Rights into Practical and Meaningful Benefits

Special statement at the Opening Ceremonies of the United Nations Permanent Forum on Indigenous Issues, 15th Session, May 9, 2016

Today, I stand before you as the Minister of Justice and Attorney General of Canada – an appointment that speaks volumes to how far our country has come but also how far we intend to go. I am also honoured to be among a record number of Indigenous members of Parliament elected last October. I believe that this represents a real change from the time when most Indigenous People were actively discouraged from participating fully in society. This past election saw Indigenous Peoples vote in record numbers.

Further, I am extremely proud to be part of a government whose leader has made a solemn commitment to fundamental change with a vision for true reconciliation with Indigenous Peoples. To this end, our Prime Minister has tasked all of his ministers to work towards rebuilding the relationship, which is set out in each of our public mandate letters, letters that state: "No relationship is more important to me and to Canada than the one with Indigenous peoples. It is time for a renewed, nation-to-nation relationship with Indigenous peoples based on recognition of rights, respect, cooperation and partnership."

That said, this is perhaps the most challenging area of public policy our government's priorities seek to address – but this work is necessary and long overdue. We must complete the unfinished business of Confederation.

Rebuilding the nation-to-nation relationship and achieving reconciliation lies at the heart of a strong Canada.

We need to find long-term solutions to decades-old problems as we seek to deconstruct our colonial legacy. Important to this work will be implementing the calls to action set out in the recent report of the Truth and Reconciliation Commission, which considered the legacy of the Indian residential schools. One of the significant challenges to this work is that, although strengthening the nation-to-nation relationship is the goal, practically speaking, the administration of Indigenous affairs in Canada is not actually organized around Indigenous Nations. For the most part, it is organized around an imposed system of governance. With respect to "Indians," this is through "bands," which are creatures of federal statute under the Indian Act, the Indian Act being the antithesis of self-government as an expression of self-determination.

Simply put, we need to move beyond the system of imposed governance.

And I am confident that we have the legal tools to do so – that for Indian, Inuit, and Métis peoples, we can and will breathe life into section 35 of Canada's Constitution, which recognizes and affirms existing Aboriginal and Treaty Rights by embracing the principles and minimum standards articulated in the United Nations Declaration on the Rights of Indigenous Peoples and guided by the dozens of court decisions that provide instruction.

The challenge moving forward, I submit, is not to fight battles already won but rather to translate these hard-fought-for rights into practical and meaningful benefits on the ground in our communities. But as any person who has worked in Indigenous communities in Canada knows, it is not easy to decolonize; it is not easy to throw off the shackles of 140 years of the Indian Act system, for example. Indigenous communities are clearly in a period of transition – of Nation building and rebuilding. Our job as the Government of Canada is to support this transition.

Tied to the fundamental work of Nation rebuilding and implementing the United Nations Declaration, one of the biggest legal questions we need to unpack is how to implement the concept of "free, prior and informed consent." The Declaration recognizes that Indigenous Peoples have both individual and collective rights. Participation in real decision making is at the heart of the Declaration's concept of free, prior, and informed consent – that Indigenous Peoples must be able to participate in making decisions that affect their lives. There are many facets to the question, differing perspectives, and a number of options. All require a new nation-to-nation relationship, reflected in our unique constitutional requirements.

So, how do we move forward? As the late Nelson Mandela taught us, beyond the necessary truth telling and healing, reconciliation actually requires laws to change and policies to be rewritten. We intend to do so in full partnership. There is a need for a national action plan in Canada, something our government has been referring to as a reconciliation framework. In accordance with the reconciliation framework, we need more effective and clear ways of recognizing Indigenous Nations and providing supports in the transition for those Nations that are ready, willing, and able to move beyond the status quo. At the same time, we need to ensure that communities continue to receive the necessary programs and services during the period of transition. This work also necessarily includes developing a new fiscal relationship with Indigenous governments.

And we do not need to reinvent the wheel completely. It is important to understand what has worked and why and to build on the success. There are already many positive steps that have been taken. Within Canada, there are modern treaties and examples of self-government – both comprehensive and sectoral. There are regional and national Indigenous institutions that support Nation rebuilding – for example, in land management and financial administration.

The time is right for meaningful and systemic change to respect and acknowledge the place of Indigenous Nations. Legitimate and strong Indigenous Nations are changing and will increasingly change the way Canada is governed, and for the better. There is room in our country for different legal traditions and ways of governing, an approach that respects diversity and supports the social and economic advancement of Indigenous Peoples as part of our evolving system of cooperative federalism and multilevel governance.

For this vision to be realized, Indigenous Peoples need to be empowered to take back control of their own lives in partnership and with the full support of all Canadians. For change to occur, communities must go through their own processes of empowerment and local transformation, through healing, rebuilding, and capacity development. In doing so, we can continue to make real progress.

And this is not just true for Indigenous Peoples in Canada. There are common challenges and opportunities for Indigenous Nations, no matter where they exist in the world. That is why the UN Permanent Forum is such an important mechanism. The bringing together of states and Indigenous Peoples to address issues of fundamental importance over the past fifteen years has made an immense impact with respect to the recognition of the rights of Indigenous Peoples.

There have been two official international decades of the world's Indigenous Peoples. I say let us make this the century of the world's Indigenous Peoples, one where Indigenous Peoples, no matter where they live, deconstruct their colonial legacy and rebuild their communities. Let us make it a century where nation-states and Indigenous Peoples work in partnership towards true reconciliation that supports strong and healthy Indigenous Peoples that are in charge of and in control of their own destinies. This, my friends, is our objective: where the Declaration and the work of this place is a means to an end and not the end in itself, the end being an improved quality of life for Indigenous Peoples with practising and thriving cultures.

UNDRIP Is the Start,
Not the Finishing Line

Address to the 37th Assembly of First Nations, July 12, 2016

This has been a momentous year and, yes, the momentum is gaining. Indigenous voices are increasingly shaping our country. Voter turnout in the 2015 federal election was up significantly – up by as much as 270 percent in some communities – and a record ten Indigenous People were elected to Parliament.

And, yes, people are taking note. For example, some of you may have seen a recent article observing how "Indigenous MPs and senators played a central role in securing passage of the new assisted dying law," bringing "unique perspective." And it is true: we did seek consensus where consensus could be achieved – very much in the spirit of Indigenous political traditions and a nonpartisan approach to decision making.

And, yes, there is momentum with the pre-inquiry consultations regarding missing and murdered Indigenous women and girls, and with beginning an early review of the Crown's position in select litigation regarding Indigenous issues.

And, yes, our government has adopted, without qualifications, the United Nations Declaration on the Rights of Indigenous Peoples.

These are all incredibly important advances. But it is still only the start.

So, National Chief Bellegarde, while I want to thank you for your optimistic and very encouraging words this morning, and for taking the time to reflect on what has transpired in the last year since Montreal, what was most important to me from your words is a signalling of the hard work that remains before us all, in particular rebuilding the nation-to-nation relationship. While we must, and will, address the social issues now – education, child welfare, and health – and consider the immediate needs with respect to closing the financial gap, in truth the social and economic gaps will never be fully closed until the foundational work of Nation rebuilding has been completed, the Indian Act gone, until Indigenous Peoples are making decisions for themselves, and until the role of the federal government has been transformed from one of designing and administering programs and services for Indigenous Peoples into one that supports self-governing Indigenous Nations in a genuine nation-to-nation relationship.

So, yes, the real work is ahead of us, and that is the message I am here to deliver today. And, in this regard, we are all very fortunate to have a Prime Minister who understands this and has tasked all of his ministers with working towards a renewed nation-to-nation relationship with Indigenous Peoples, based on "recognition of rights, respect, co-operation and partnership." So I want to talk about the nation-to-nation relationship and share some thoughts on how we can focus our efforts to collectively set in place a course of action over the coming months that ensures we can turn all the good words, the goodwill, and the golden opportunity we have into meaningful progress with practical and discernable benefits on the ground within Indigenous communities – to undertake transformative change.

And I challenge the critics that say it cannot be done, those who, on the one hand, say the government is not serious or sincere and, on the other, say that Indigenous Peoples do not have what it will take, or the resolve, or that the task is too great. And I make this challenge confident in the knowledge that there is no one in this room who would suggest that decolonization is easy; and that we all appreciate that trust, especially where trust did not exist before, must be earned; and that it can just as easily be lost; and that we all understand that the stakes are high, incredibly high. We are talking about the lives of future generations of Indigenous children within Canada, about the very survival of our distinct cultures and ancient languages, about a way of life.

Moving forward, our government's principled approach to a nation-to-nation relationship based on recognition does raise some very fundamental questions that must be answered in order to proceed. First and foremost, it raises the question, What are the Indigenous Nations that are to be recognized? That is, how will you define yourselves as Nations? What are the structures through which you will deliver programs and services? And, then, what will your relationship with Canada, with your neighbours, and with other Indigenous Nations look like? How will you resolve your differences between and amongst yourselves?

In answering these questions, I think we can all agree that the federally imposed Indian Act is not the answer, even though it is, as a result of the colonial legacy, necessarily a starting point for conversations in communities where the Indian Act system is, in most cases, currently the primary system of administration in place. Even though it is a system that reflects an impoverished notion of governance, one that is fundamentally inconsistent with the United Nations Declaration.

Let me explore this thought further. The seventh preambular paragraph in the UNDRIP speaks to promoting the inherent rights of Indigenous Peoples, which derive from their political, economic, and social structures – that is, not those imposed by the state, of which the Indian Act is a case in point. Article 3 says Indigenous Peoples have a right to self-determination and, by virtue of that right, to freely pursue their economic, social, and cultural development. And Article 5 says Indigenous Peoples have the right to maintain and strengthen their distinct political, legal, economic, social, and cultural institutions while retaining their right to participate fully, if they so choose, in the political, economic, social, and cultural life of the state.

So, again, it raises the question, What are the political, economic, and social structures that the federal government should recognize and that the UNDRIP speaks to, and what is the relationship of those institutions to the federal machinery of government? As we all know, there is no simple answer. It is, unfortunately, not as simple as just ripping up the Indian Act. Although, if we are speaking openly, adopting the UNDRIP should really require us to do so. But, in so doing, we would also create legal and economic uncertainty during the period of transition.

How we deal with the existing administrative structures on reserve, including the Indian Act mechanisms that already exist to support the transition, must be carefully considered. There are already significant infrastructure and steps towards economic improvement on many reserves, so we have to be very careful about the new mechanisms that we put in place – to build on our success. At the same time, we also have to be mindful of the vested interests in the status quo that are resistant to change, not to mention the citizens of the Nations who may be afraid of change and more comfortable with the devil they know than the devil they do not. But this is the challenge of Nation rebuilding, something that those of us who have been dealing with these issues for years fully understand and embrace.

So, as much as I would tomorrow like to cast into the fire of history the Indian Act so that the Nations can be reborn in its ashes, this is not a practical option, which is why simplistic approaches, such as adopting the UNDRIP as being Canadian law, are unworkable and, respectfully, a political distraction to undertaking the hard work required to actually implement it. What we need is an efficient process of transition that lights a fire under the process of decolonization but does so in a controlled manner that respects where Indigenous communities are in terms of rebuilding. As was described to me by one Chief when I was BC Regional Chief, rather than popping the balloon that is the Indian Act, we need to let the air out slowly in a controlled and deliberate manner, slowly until it is all gone, and when it is all out, what replaces it will be strong and healthy First Nation governments, governments that design and deliver their own programs and services.

This approach is consistent with Article 38 of the UNDRIP, which sets out that the role of the state, in consultation and cooperation with Indigenous Peoples, is to take the appropriate measures to achieve the ends of the Declaration. Accordingly, the way the UNDRIP will get implemented in Canada will be through a mixture of legislation, policy, and action initiated and taken by Indigenous Nations themselves. Ultimately, the UNDRIP will be articulated through the constitutional framework of section 35.

So, what are the improved or new mechanisms we need to support the nation-to-nation relationship? What legislation or changes to policy do we need now and in the future, to create the legal and political space for Indigenous Peoples to move forward, to breathe life into section 35?

What the federal government can do now is begin the process to recognize your Nations and your legitimate institutions of government. What we can do, in full partnership, is to facilitate the transition, to set us on an irreversible path of action and to develop a national reconciliation framework with improved and new mechanisms to guide this transition to rebuilding strong, self-determining Nations with practising and thriving cultures. This includes mechanisms to negotiate modern treaties under new mandates as well as other constructive arrangements that will provide a clear and predictable path for Indigenous Peoples and governments for the exercise of decision making and governance. It means supporting Nation building in the context of historic treaties and, where there are no treaties, respecting the proper title holders. It means creating new mechanisms to facilitate self-government beyond the Indian Act band.

And we need to get moving on developing these mechanisms as soon as possible and, yes, this work will be controversial. But it is absolutely necessary, and it cannot take multiple generations. We do not have time. Incredibly, by some accounts, at the current rate, negotiating our way out of the dysfunction of the Indian Act system using existing mechanisms would take hundreds of years. This is not acceptable.

To truly celebrate the 150th anniversary of Canada next year, I would very much like to be able to come back to the 2017 AFN Assembly knowing we have a jointly developed plan put in place and with the work well under way to develop and implement the mechanisms to support the transition in this, what some have called "the age of recognition." We simply cannot waste time on reinventing the wheel or replicating reports of yesterday – we must act with conviction and determination.

As a proud Indigenous person as well as a proud Canadian, I know that my future and the future of the generations to come is inextricably tied to the success of the project of creating a stronger Canada that is inclusive and respects diversity – a post-nation-state that recognizes pluralism and a system of government that supports this objective.

Strong Indigenous Nations are a part of this vision. Legitimate and strong Indigenous Nations have already begun to change the way Canada is governed for the better and will continue to do so. There is room in our country for different legal traditions and ways of governing, for an approach that respects diversity and equality and supports the social and economic advancement of Indigenous Peoples as part of our evolving system of co-operative federalism and multilevel governance. It is what distinguishes Canada as a nation from other nations of the world, where ethnic tensions threaten cohesion and, with it, social and economic stability – indeed, human progress.

Accordingly, there is no place within today's Canada for governments to deny the place of Indigenous Peoples to participate fully in decisions that directly and significantly affect them or where rights require action or jurisdiction to be respected. And to this end, the nation-to-nation relationship is so critical. Where land-use decisions are being made that affect Indigenous Peoples, the legitimate and recognized governments of those peoples must be able to participate in shared decision making with other levels of government. For me, this is how free, prior, and informed consent is operationalized.

I see the role of my department in this period of transition as one of legal facilitation of recognition and reconciliation – to work to lay out the constitutional and legal foundations within government and then to facilitate building the tools and processes needed to bridge between the present and that future state. On this note, the previous government enacted a suite of legislation that I, along with many others and you, have said is inconsistent with developing a nation-to-nation relationship, and as we develop the mechanisms to the transition we will have to reconsider this legislation. And, of course, there will continue to be litigation between Indigenous Peoples and the Crown. Accordingly, my role as Minister of Justice and Attorney General is to ensure that the Charter is upheld and that the legal positions taken by the Crown in court are consistent with the commitments and values of our government with respect to the evolving nation-to-nation relationship with Indigenous Peoples.

By way of conclusion, let me leave you with these final thoughts.

Now is the time. The political and legal ducks are aligned. There is a friendly government, but we need your solutions. As a government, we are not going to impose solutions. With your leadership, we can and will make enormous progress. There is no need to refight battles that have already been won. Limited resources, time, and energy have to be expended on building, not fighting; on creating, not destroying; on empowering, not protest. Pressing social issues must be addressed now. But Nations need to be ready to assume jurisdiction and the responsibilities that come with it. And while the federal government has a crucial supporting role to play, the hard work is going to be in the community. As I said in the House of Commons during the Emergency Attawapiskat debate, only the colonized can actually decolonize. No one else can do it for you.

Defining the Path of Reconciliation
through Section 35

Address to the Continuing Legal Education Society of British Columbia, Aboriginal Law Conference, November 25, 2016

We have been in government for just over a year now, and over the course of that year, it has often been repeated that no relationship is more important to Prime Minister Trudeau and our government than the one with Indigenous Peoples, to the point where I think there are very few people in this country who aren't aware of this. To facilitate the relationship, each of the ministers is mandated with fostering reconciliation – that is, prioritizing the need for a renewed nation-to-nation relationship with Indigenous Peoples based on recognition of rights, respect, cooperation, and partnership. Powerful words. And not surprisingly, expectations are high, and so they should be.

And with such high expectations, it is also not surprising that there are some who are now questioning our government's commitment because progress has not been seen as occurring perhaps quite fast enough. But change takes time. Rome was not built in a day, and neither is rebuilding Indigenous Nations. I can assure you that the commitment of our government and my commitment have not wavered and remain strong. And as I have said elsewhere, the legacy of this government will, in a very large measure, be determined by the ongoing relationship between the Crown and Indigenous Peoples.

So there should be no misunderstanding. Change is coming. This is real; this is not a dress rehearsal. When our government says we are approaching the relationship based on recognition, we mean it. And this requires a new way of doing business, both for government and for Indigenous Peoples. As such, we are very much in a period of transition. And the transition is not easy. It is messy, it is not simple to break free from dysfunctional colonial systems epitomized by the Indian Act to a true nation-to-nation relationship, one based on recognition of First Peoples and not one centred around federally imposed band administration and power. In this transition, we all have a role to play and we all have responsibilities.

In my remarks in 2010, speaking then as Regional Chief, I suggested that for many of our people, Indigenous Peoples who live on reserve, important legal instruments such as the United Nations Declaration on the Rights of Indigenous Peoples and section 35 of the Canadian Constitution and the reams of Aboriginal Title and Rights cases flowing from it mean very little to Indigenous People who are struggling to make ends meet, as they try to make do with the backward political chaos of Indian Act government and/or the confusion and contradictory relationships Indigenous Peoples still have within Canada as both colonial authority and a partner. I talked about how, in some ways, it was easier in the past to divorce the actual reality of our Indian Act community lives from the fight for legal recognition of rights and title, where our leaders would go to Ottawa, Victoria, or Vancouver championing section 35 and fighting vociferously for self-government knowing that the rank and file in our communities, if asked, would vote against self-government, the majority of them afraid of life beyond the Indian Act, coupled with the insidious dependency on the federal government.

In this context, I questioned then what would happen if we, as Indigenous Peoples, got everything we were asking for, including the right to self-government. At the time, I observed there still had not been a declaration of title. Today, of course, we now do in *Tsilhqot'in* (2014). I asked: Would we – again, remember, speaking as a First Nations representative – be prepared to govern the day after a declaration was granted, a challenging but most welcome reality for the Tŝilhqot'in, who are dealing with this at this moment?

And today, there is a new reality for all. It is not only a changed legal landscape but also a political one. And as hard as it might be for some to believe recognition is actually coming, let me assure you it is, with all the questions that this raises and hard work ahead to operationalize it. And while we cannot know exactly how it will all unfold, and, certainly, we do not have all the answers at the outset, the nation-to-nation relationship will, I know, fundamentally transform our country. It will change Canada for the better moving into a postcolonial world. It will be transformative. It is how we breathe life into section 35 and actually implement the United Nations Declaration on the Rights of Indigenous Peoples. Interestingly, a lot of commentary has been made about my statements earlier this year at the Assembly of First Nations in Niagara Falls, where I said that "simplistic approaches such as adopting the United Nations Declaration as being Canadian law are unworkable and, respectfully, a political distraction to undertaking the hard work actually required to implement it back home in communities."

Let me offer a few reflections on my statement. First, and to be very clear, and contrary to what might have been posted in social media or mis-reported in the media, our government has endorsed the United Nations Declaration unequivocally. What I was saying, though, is that you cannot simply incorporate the UNDRIP word for word into federal statute. Unfortunately, this has become politicized. The critical work of reconciliation, of which implementing the United Nations Declaration is a central part, must be above the daily push and pull of political choices, discourse, and expediency. True reconciliation has to be above politics or, rather, it has to be about a different order of politics, an order of politics that is dignified and that commits us all – Indigenous and non-Indigenous Canadians alike – to chart a future together, to be reconciled together, to make Canada whole together. This is because reconciliation demands so much of all of us – the Crown, Indigenous governments, and civil society.

Reconciliation requires putting colonialism into the past, including beyond the Indian Act. It demands rebuilding Indigenous government and communities and closing the sociocultural gap between Indigenous and non-Indigenous peoples. It involves recognizing the Indigenous relationship with the land; respecting treaties and Aboriginal Title and Rights; and building new structures and making decisions in new ways. It is the politics of nation building. In other words, reconciliation involves fundamental changes in the ways of talking, acting, and relating that we all have to be a part of – Indigenous and non-Indigenous, for many generations – and transforming laws, policies, structures, and processes that we have taken for granted for too long. We must all be nation builders. There is no single piece of legislation that can accomplish this.

While new and changed legislation will be required and will take place, we need that and far more. Implementing the United Nations Declaration on the Rights of Indigenous Peoples will require an interlocking set of new laws, policies, institutions, structures, and patterns of relations. We must pursue those changes comprehensively. We cannot afford to invest our focus, time, and energy on one initiative or approach that only meets a small part of the challenge or gives a false sense of comfort that, really, change has occurred. For too long, small steps and initiatives on the path of reconciliation have been misrepresented as major shifts. Now is the time, working collaboratively with Indigenous Peoples, to deliberately and systematically design and implement the major changes that are needed to be transformative. Recognition and building the nation-to-nation relationship will do this.

Lastly, it is important that we always keep in mind the relationship between the United Nations Declaration and section 35 of the Canadian Constitution. Section 35, when it was adopted, was intended to complete the critical unfinished promise of achieving reconciliation between Indigenous Peoples and the Crown. For that reason, political conferences and work was to be done following the adoption of section 35 to achieve that goal. That work did not unfold as intended. As a result, Indigenous Peoples had to continue the long, expensive, and arduous path of using the courts to define how section 35 will achieve reconciliation. That work of defining the path of reconciliation through section 35 is ongoing. The United Nations Declaration now accelerates and provides a framework for this work, by working together at the political and community levels to implement it.

We are fulfilling the intention and the promise of section 35 while ensuring we are upholding the minimum standards in the Declaration and the fundamental human rights of Indigenous Peoples. Central to the work of reconciliation is moving from conflict to collaboration and considering how we can structure our legal processes to better serve this ultimate goal. This requires grappling with how we play our roles as lawyers, when and how we choose to use the courts, and what we do and say when we get there. As lawyers, we need to consider this question from the perspective of "what are the objectives of our clients?" and interpreting the instructions from them and providing advice. Recognition of rights has never been the end objective in itself for Indigenous Peoples, I would submit. The end objective has always been to ultimately improve the lives of Indigenous Peoples, translating rights into actual practical benefits, ensuring that they are operationalized on the ground in communities.

Fifty years ago, when there was limited or no recognition of Aboriginal Title and Rights, the advice of lawyers working for Indigenous clients was simple: make a claim for the land, resources, and governance based on the fact that no treaty had been entered into and that Nation's land had not been ceded to the Crown. Central to the work of reconciliation is moving from conflict to collaboration and considering how we can structure our legal processes to better serve this ultimate goal. This requires grappling with how we play our role as lawyers, when and how we choose to go to court, and what we do and say when we get there. As lawyers, of course, we have responsibilities to faithfully and diligently serve our clients, but when working in Aboriginal law (the Crown context), this service can be rendered in different ways that advance or hinder the work of reconciliation, both in that specific set of relationships and more broadly in society as a whole.

For far too long, the federal government has taken positions in court that have not been aligned with reconciliation. These positions at various times and in various ways have been rooted in notions that Indigenous Peoples were uncivilized, disorganized, without laws and governments and, in some instances, did not even exist as distinct peoples. In a word, it was all about denial. One thing we are now doing in my department is to begin applying the lens of reconciliation to all positions we take and in the choices we make on the road to and within litigation. This is why we are beginning to find ways to recognize Indigenous Peoples and Aboriginal and Treaty Rights, including title, to create new space for solutions to be found in how we interpret the law, present the facts or frame the issues and, in some instances, seek to move matters altogether. And this is not easy. It takes time, and much more needs to be done. But the work has begun, and some significant changes have already been seen.

The Aboriginal Bar also has an important role to play in moving reconciliation forward. As more space emerges to find constructive solutions and ways forward that may move us out of the courts, the Aboriginal Bar has to creatively take advantage and use that space. Similarly, just as we are seeking to do in my department, in situations where we do end up in court, members of the Aboriginal Bar may also consider how to frame the issues and positions in disputes in ways that focus all of us and the court on the core issues in the dispute and make the proceedings more effective for everyone involved.

Beyond this, we all need to grapple more with the question of how. For example, we can all agree that recognition is fundamental to reconciliation. What we need to spend more time considering is how recognition is translated and implemented into tangible and real ways on the ground between governments, in communities, and across Canada. For those of you in the Aboriginal Bar, what does recognition look like in the relationship between the Crown and the Nations you represent? What does it mean for how decisions are made; for the structures we have; for the ways in which the Nations' government and the federal government are structured, operating, and interacting; for the economic relationship of the Nation and all Canadians to resources of territory. And are you, in fact, representing a Nation, as contemplated in the nation-to-nation relationship, that is the proper title and rights holder?

It's important to always advance principled legal positions. We now need to be ready to articulate in real ways what the application of those principles will look like so we can work together to move from abstract frameworks for reconciliation to real action. This is a responsibility we all share as lawyers working in this context. And it is in this regard, and now speaking certainly as the Minister of Justice, that I see my central role, and not just ensuring that the Crown's positions in court are principled but that our country's laws and policies actually change, based on recognition to support the real action of reconciliation. And there are numerous laws and policies that need to change and new ones to be developed. Legal and political reconciliation in furtherance of the nation-to-nation relationship is a national project that requires significant coordination and commitment at the highest level of government. For all of us at the highest level, the United Nations Declaration provides the framework for reconciliation, setting minimum standards, and is instructive on how we develop our own made-in-Canada framework for reconciliation, reflecting our history and our unique legal and constitutional framework. Above all else, this framework for reconciliation must be grounded in a commitment to principles. Those principles should not only be grounded in the law but should also demonstrate a commitment to go beyond existing legal obligations and to strengthen the nation-to-nation relationship.

Transformative change must comply with the Crown's constitutional obligations, but it must go beyond them. Transformative change requires the government to demonstrate leadership under section 35 so that the Crown, and not only the courts, are seen to be leaders in realizing reconciliation. For example, a strong commitment to a renewed nation-to-nation relationship between the government and Indigenous Peoples requires a principled approach based on the recognition and implementation of the inherent rights of Indigenous Peoples. It should also acknowledge the centrality of the honour of the Crown in all processes. It should understand that treaties and agreements and other constructive arrangements between the Crown and Indigenous Peoples are acts of reconciliation based on mutual recognition and respect, and that mechanisms for reconciliation must be developed in partnership with Indigenous Peoples. These are all key principles that need to guide Crown action.

With respect to specific mechanisms to be developed to facilitate the renewed nation-to-nation relationship, there are currently no simple mechanisms for recognition in Canada that support the transition away from the colonial-imposed systems of administration – for example, the Indian Act. This is obviously not acceptable and clearly demands a more concerted effort by government, with new legislative tools and other mechanisms to support Nation rebuilding. This is something our government is committed to developing in partnership with Indigenous Peoples. And I cannot stress this enough. As we proceed, based on recognition, it is absolutely imperative that Indigenous groups propose solutions as to how to manage the transition from the imposed systems of government and administration. As a government, we are not going to impose solutions. And while I'm aware of solutions that are already working (but where mandates need to change and processes tweaked), I am aware of others that have been proposed over the years but never acted upon, such as recognition legislation or the establishment of specialized dispute-resolution bodies.

I know that there are other solutions and ideas out there. For example, I know some Indigenous groups are looking to work together to advance the development of new Indigenous institutions that respect but transcend the Indigenous Nation. For me, personally, the work of developing strong and appropriate Indigenous governance is the work of Nation rebuilding that really excites me, because, as an Indigenous person, I know it is essential to ensuring thriving and practising Indigenous cultures reflective of our Indigenous legal traditions.

Indeed, Indigenous laws and legal orders are central to the work of reconciliation and creating new nation-to-nation relationships. Both section 35 of the Constitution and the United Nations Declaration speak to this. And many of the Truth and Reconciliation calls to action touch on the need to understand and engage Indigenous laws. Canada has always been a country with dimensions of legal pluralism – the coming together of different legal orders that learn to coexist and operate together within our constitutional framework. This was true at the founding of the country almost 150 years ago in relation to our common law and civil law heritage. Expressing dimensions of legal pluralism is a challenge we must now meet in relation to Indigenous laws as well. Indigenous governments, the Crown, law schools, and the bar all have roles and responsibilities to play in relation to how Indigenous legal orders come to be further understood and expressed in Canada.

Indigenous Nations across the country are at various stages and in different processes of rebuilding their governments. This is essential work they must do as part of ushering in an era of new relationships where self-government and recognition and the exercise of Indigenous jurisdiction will steadily increase. Nations must tackle the hard work of increasing their governance capacity. This includes reinvigorating and expressing in diverse and new ways the laws and legal orders that Indigenous Peoples have relied on for countless generations. They must also undertake the work of expressing their laws and their application in a contemporary world. The Crown has the opportunity to seek out and create the appropriate space for the operation and application of Indigenous laws and legal orders through changes in our own existing laws and by creating new models of relations. This requires moving beyond the practice of denying the operation of Indigenous laws and starting the work of creating a pattern of legal pluralism that recognizes them and includes their role.

Law schools and the bar have vital roles to play. We need to systematically build understanding about Indigenous laws – how they operate, how they fit into the constitutional fabric of Canada, and how their application is part of the work of reconciliation. Law schools should continue to rise to the challenge of training new lawyers equipped with the knowledge of these matters and the roles they play, as lawyers, in ensuring they are respected. In my position, I have been privileged to see this happening across the country. Similarly, the bar as a whole has to build opportunities for gaining deep understanding of Indigenous laws relevant in various ways to all areas of contemporary legal practices. And note that in the new open and transparent process our government has adopted for judicial appointments, to ensure greater diversity on the bench, we will strongly consider candidates with knowledge of Indigenous legal traditions.

In practice, when considering the way Indigenous laws and legal orders contribute to legal pluralism in Canada, there are many areas of the law to consider, as there are many different legal traditions reflecting the diversity of Indigenous Peoples within Canada. There are unique Indigenous systems of land tenure and land holding, with different rules of how property is passed on and rules of descent. Nations have different traditions when it comes to how decisions are made within governing bodies, often with special rules for certain groups – for example, the rule of the Matriarchs and hereditary Chiefs. In the area of family law, there may be special rules with respect to the raising and responsibilities for children that extend beyond biological parents. In some cases, Indigenous legal traditions are something that all Canadians can learn and benefit from and that can have wider application than simply to the specific Indigenous Peoples whose legal order it is – for example, with respect to how disputes are resolved.

A case in point is in the area of sentencing. Measures such as restorative justice and sentencing circles are already providing off-ramps to the criminal justice system in Canada and leading to lower incarceration rates and recidivism rates for nonviolent offences. This is, in fact, Restorative Justice Week, and I would like to acknowledge that British Columbia has been a leader in bringing restorative justice measures forward. Indigenous legal traditions will, I am sure, increasingly have a positive impact on our country as the process of reconciliation unfolds.

So, let me say this. Today, we truly have an opportunity to develop a nation-to-nation relationship that will ensure that Indigenous Peoples take their rightful place within Confederation in our evolving system of multi-level governance and cooperative federalism. And, as part of this Indigenous Nation rebuilding, Indigenous laws and legal orders are going to play an increasingly important role in our country's legal mosaic. As someone who was raised in the laws of our Big House, and now being where I am today, I can appreciate both the importance of ensuring Indigenous legal orders, including those of my people, the Kwakwa̱ka̱'wakw, and ensuring legal pluralism. Through reconciliation and the promotion of legal pluralism, I am incredibly excited about the prospects of how our institutions of governance in Canada will become the stronger for it.

In my opinion, the nation-to-nation relationship and the resurgence of Indigenous governance, based on Indigenous legal orders, will, over the next generation, change for the better the way Canada is governed, not only in transforming Indigenous Nations, but our country as a whole. And as Indigenous People take back control of their lives, the federation is strengthened. We are helping to ensure that we have a Canada that I think all Canadians aspire to live in – a country based on shared values and principles that we have spent years as a nation fostering, creating a fair, caring, and compassionate society that confirms our place on this planet

Indigenous Rights Are Human Rights

Adapted from address to "Constitution 150 Conference," March 10, 2017

Today, as we consider the 150th anniversary of Canada, the theme of my remarks is patriation, the recognition of rights, and reconciliation. The idea that the recognition of rights accompanied patriation is a familiar one. The Charter of Rights and Freedoms that accompanied Canada's constitutional independence is the obvious manifestation of that recognition. And it has been transformative. Indeed, in many ways it defines our country. When asked what Canadians value most about Canada, after health care, it is the Charter.

However, for Indigenous Peoples – the 150 year celebration has, for obvious reasons, evoked mixed reactions. On the one hand, it is hard to celebrate the past 150 years – a history of colonization, denial, and failed promises. But on the other, there is a renewed hope for a better and more inclusive Canada over the next 150 years. This is because the recognition of rights that was brought about with patriation has been only partial, for the guarantee in section 35 of the Constitution that the rights of Indigenous People "are hereby recognized and affirmed" has not been the reality of Canada's relationship with Indigenous Peoples. Despite section 35, Indigenous Peoples have still had to spend the last thirty-five years using the courts to prove that their rights exist and that governments should respect those rights. The end result is that we have spent more time in conflict rather than in a nation-to-nation relationship grounded in recognition and respect, which a rights-based approach demands and as is reflected more generally in the principles of civil society that the very idea of the Charter evokes.

I will return to this subject, but first I would like to reflect on the 35th anniversary of the Charter of Rights and Freedoms in Canada's 150th year. The Charter is internationally renowned and continues to be full of promise today. The story of our Charter begins not in 1982 but in the global recognition of rights that followed the systematic denial and violation of those same rights. The Second World War and the Universal Declaration of Human Rights represent both the worst and the best of the human condition, both the most frightening and the most promising illustration of our capacity for human endeavour.

The Universal Declaration of Human Rights sought to affirm the universality of human rights against the odds of history and geography – an affirmation in one time, at one place, for all time, and for all people everywhere. The success of this endeavour before the UN General Assembly in December 1948 rested on its ability to incorporate different visions of freedom or, as French philosopher Jacques Maritain poetically put it, "many different kinds of music [can] be played on the document's thirty strings."

The initial draft of the Declaration was prepared by the first director of the UN Secretariat's Human Rights Division, a Canadian whose name will be known to many – John Humphrey. Humphrey instructed his staff "to study all the world's existing constitutions and rights instruments" to prepare a draft document recognizing universal rights. The creation of the Declaration proceeded from the local as it aspired to the universal – national and regional attempts to set out rights and freedoms for selected communities informed the grander appeal to universality for all of the world's communities. Quite an ambition. Perhaps because of this approach, Humphrey, when questioned on what philosophy had guided him in setting out a first draft document of universal rights, responded that the draft was based on "no philosophy whatsoever."

I do not think Humphrey meant that the very idea of human rights – their universality, their indivisibility, their inalienability, their inviolability – is without philosophical authority. On the contrary, Humphrey sought to insulate the Declaration from the charge that it was motivated and articulated from the perspective of any one governing philosophy or worldview. Arguably, the only philosophical disposition or worldview nakedly inconsistent with the Universal Declaration was one that would deny the very idea of rights. In this way, Humphrey captured how the success of the Universal Declaration was to affirm rights common to humankind, to affirm that each right was to be read in relation to every other, and to do so in a manner that would be acceptable to the world's many political communities. By doing so, it became a new collective and truly global worldview.

It is a success that is not to be underestimated. The vote to adopt the Declaration before the UN General Assembly in December 1948 was unanimous. There was not a single dissenting vote. To this day, the Universal Declaration remains an iconic affirmation of our capacity for human good. It remains, too, a ready reminder of the many ways in which human rights are declared for everyone, but not everywhere recognized.

After its passage, the Universal Declaration required a renewed effort by Canada to recognize rights in our laws and policies. The Canada of 1948 was not without its human rights successes, but nor was it without its human rights failures. Despite Canada's support for the Declaration being based on strong foundations, we were quite a different country than we are today. Before the 1960 Canadian Bill of Rights, there was no pan-Canadian recognition of rights, no pan-Canadian affirmation of the Universal Declaration in Canadian law. Our rights and freedoms were not recognized in any supreme law. The fate of the Canadian Bill of Rights is well known to everyone. While an important part of our human rights history, it was also not transformative. Despite the significance of 1960, it is not a year that stands out in Canadian history as the turning point for the recognition of rights.

In contrast to 1960, the year 1982 does stand out as transformative in Canadian history. It stands out as the year marking the recognition of rights in our constitutional order. It is a year known for many milestones: patriation, a constitutional amendment formula, constitutional independence, the birth of another major constitutional instrument, and the renaming of our founding constitutional instrument so that our Confederation Constitution would no longer be known as the colonial "British North

America Act." The year 1982 is known, too, for the promise captured in section 35 of the Constitution Act.

But for many Canadians, 1982 is remembered above all else for the Charter of Rights and Freedoms – 1982's defining moment. It is a reputation that the Charter has earned over time. It is a reputation grounded in the Charter's success to do what the Canadian Bill of Rights failed to do – that is, to inspire and instill a culture of rights within Canada's governing institutions and within Canada's peoples. That culture of rights has been a culture of the recognition of rights.

The Charter is Canada's Universal Declaration – our vision of freedom within the human family or, to paraphrase Jacques Maritain, it is Canada's music played on the Declaration's thirty strings. Many of the rights and freedoms guaranteed by the Charter are formulated in language that tracks very closely the wording in the Declaration: the fundamental freedoms to expression, association, religion and conscience, and peaceful assembly; the rights to life, liberty, and security of the person; criminal justice rights; and equality rights. Other aspects of our Charter signal the special emphasis that we – as a country – place on the recognition of rights: our official language rights, our minority language educational rights, and our commitment to multiculturalism.

For some, that special emphasis is not a candidate for universal affirmation. Certainly, for a time, some of these rights were saddled with a restrictive interpretation, a reading that limited their scope on account of a "political pact" understanding of their nature. This reading was in contrast to the broad and generous interpretation awarded to the more universalist rights in the Charter. That understanding has waned. In fact, it was never a contender. It was never true to the Universal Declaration itself, which captures, in its twenty-second article, the complex story of individuality and community: "Everyone, as a member of society ... is entitled to realization ... of the economic, social and cultural rights indispensable for his dignity and the free development of his personality."

The closing thought of the Declaration's twenty-second article is powerful: "Economic, social, and cultural rights are indispensable for dignity and the free development of one's personality." Consider the relationship of the individual to the community captured by this reference. This relationship is perhaps the richest question of political philosophy. And the Declaration signals that it is indispensable for the dignity of individuals that they and their rights be situated in community. It is a conception of rights that is familiar to Indigenous Peoples.

So it is perhaps Canada's special contribution to human rights instruments that we began our Charter with a clause that affirms that special relationship between the community and the individual. Our Charter's first section signals that the very understanding of rights must be one that is situated socially. It is an understanding that should not be distracted by readings of section 1 of the Charter that suggest that governments have licence to violate rights and freedoms. No government has that authority, even if many have purported to exercise it. The justification for positioning this clause first in our Charter, first in the constitutional instrument that marks our patriation, is to pair the recognition of rights with the free and democratic society in which they are recognized.

Over the past thirty-five years, the transformative change brought about by the Charter is in very large part owed to the leadership of our courts. Yes, there are those that may be critical, but the reputation of our Charter as a human rights instrument is a result of the jurisprudence that now underpins it, and that jurisprudence is the result of individuals and groups seeking recognition of their rights before our courts and of the courts, in turn, finding the balance that defines Canada. In many ways, this distinguishes us from other nations and makes our country special in a world where rights and freedoms seem to be in a period of global retraction.

There is no question that the past thirty-five years of judicial application of the Charter has strengthened our laws and our policies and made our country better. It has affirmed not only the philosophical priority of rights but also their legal priority by putting the authors of laws and policies to the test of justification: Can our laws and policies be justified as being consistent with the recognition of rights?

Judicial leadership has been the defining success of the past thirty-five years of our Charter. The success of our Charter over the next thirty-five years will, I hope, be measured by political leadership. The success or failure of the Charter's next thirty-five transformative years will be measured by the ability of political leaders to demonstrate that a recognition-of-rights approach guides the development of our laws and our policies.

Since my appointment as Minister of Justice and Attorney General of Canada, I have sought to frame my role and my responsibility as "ambassador of the Charter." It is a way of signalling that the Charter is, for our government, not a constraint on the actions we take under threat of judicial review but rather a guide for a recognition-of-rights culture within the activity of government. Much of this work is quiet and out of view. It is the work of policy development. It is the work of providing legal advice on the Charter to cabinet and my ministerial colleagues. It is the work of developing and shaping memoranda to cabinet.

The evidence of our success in adopting a recognition-of-rights approach will be measured by our outcomes. Simply put, do our laws and our policies reflect our commitment to the Charter? Even if much of our recognition-of-rights work is necessarily out of view, in the spirit of accountability and transparency some of it is, and must be, publicly communicated, and is done so proudly.

Earlier this year, the Minister of Canadian Heritage and I announced the re-establishment of a renewed, modernized, and expanded Court Challenges Program. Government funding for Charter challenges is a way of signalling political responsibility for the Charter, as we recognize that not all of our laws and policies are always as they should be. Not all Canadians have an equal chance to have their day in court, and sometimes those that most need to bring a challenge are the least able to do so. The Court Challenges Program seeks to remove some of the economic barriers faced by those seeking recognition of their rights.

One of the initiatives I undertook upon taking office as the Minister of Justice, and of which I am particularly proud, is the use of "Charter Statements." For each bill I have tabled in the house, I have tabled an accompanying Charter Statement, which outlines how a recognition-of-rights approach has guided the development of each new legislative initiative. This is a very powerful way of demonstrating how the Charter is top of mind in the development of legislative initiatives. It is transparent and instructs informed debate. Each Charter Statement aims to highlight for public and parliamentary consideration and debate key Charter rights and freedoms that are engaged in my department's legislative initiatives. The political leadership that will guide the next thirty-five years of the Charter and beyond requires an actively engaged government and Parliament. I hope that the tabling of Charter Statements will help ensure a recognition-of-rights culture in all of our legislative work.

Reflecting on the conduct of the Attorney General in Charter litigation, let me say this. In reviewing Canada's litigation strategy in Charter cases, I have sought to act in a principled manner, mindful of the special constitutional position of the Attorney General, who is both a member of the executive and the chief law officer of the Crown, mandated to defend Parliament's legislative record. A principled approach has been necessary, especially when laws adopted under a previous Parliament are challenged in court and again especially when our Government has committed to repealing the impugned provisions. The question asked is, Should I concede the Charter challenge?

In conceiving of my responsibilities, I have identified and am following six principles that I believe should guide the Attorney General in Charter cases:

1. *The principle of constitutionalism and the rule of law.* The Attorney General must uphold and adhere to the Charter. Where the Attorney General concludes that there is no viable argument in favour of a law's Charter compliance, she should concede a Charter claim. However, it should be noted that the Charter itself invites some nuance here, as there are three possible places for Charter concessions: whether a right is limited, whether the limitation is justified, and what the remedy should be.

2. *The principle of parliamentary democracy.* The Attorney General is responsible for upholding laws passed by Canada's democratically elected legislature until they are changed by Parliament or declared unconstitutional by a court. As a member of the executive branch, the Attorney General should not undermine parliamentary democracy by readily conceding the unconstitutionality of laws that have been approved by Parliament. The Attorney General may therefore defend the Charter

compliance of federal legislation at the same time that her government promises to amend or repeal the challenged legislation through the parliamentary process.

3. *The principle of adjudication.* The only institutions that can authoritatively determine questions of law are courts. In fulfilling their duty, courts are assisted by full and fair argument by counsel, each putting forward the best case for and against the compliance of federal law with the Charter. Unqualified concessions by the Attorney General on constitutional questions may frustrate the courts' ability to arrive at informed constitutional conclusions.

4. *The principle of continuity.* The Crown's legal position, as advanced by the Attorney General, must be coherent and consistent across changes in government. While a new Attorney General may change a previous government's litigation strategy, any changes must be informed by her evaluation of what is in the public interest and not in the partisan interest.

5. *The principle of consistent application of the Charter.* Charter rights should be interpreted and applied coherently across the country. And yet, a finding of unconstitutionality by a court in one province or territory has effect only in that province or territory. A decision by the Attorney General not to appeal a finding of unconstitutionality to the Supreme Court of Canada could therefore result in the inconsistent application of the Charter. The Attorney General may therefore appeal a court's ruling on a Charter question in order to ensure a pan-Canadian determination of the law.

6. *The principle of access to justice.* Litigation is expensive. Where an issue in dispute is discrete and limited to the parties before the courts, access to justice may be served by reserving scarce judicial resources for matters that are the subject of broader legal disputes. The Attorney General in these cases should seek to settle Charter litigation if she shares the legal conclusion of the claimant. In other cases, where a judicial

decision may have immediate or broader importance, access to justice may favour the continuation of litigation so that the issue can be decisively resolved in a public forum.

The interplay of these six principles will not always favour the same litigation positions. But I hope that they illustrate why, even for the ambassador of the Charter, litigation positions invite questions of deep constitutional strategy even in those instances when the Attorney General may share the Charter conclusions of claimants.

Which brings me back to the theme with which I began: reconciliation with Indigenous Peoples and the unfinished work of this country – work not completed by Confederation or patriation. The Crown's relationship with Indigenous Peoples predates both of our two great constitutional moments. In that pre-Confederation period, while there were some instances of treaty making, and at times some other constructive patterns between peoples, there were also significant wrongs and injustices. A legacy was left of massive work that still had to be done in order for proper relations between the original inhabitants of this land and settlers to live in harmony and build a shared future of mutual interdependence. This massive work was not achieved and was further complicated by colonial attitudes and structures, by disease and beliefs in the superiority and inferiority of different groups of people. Confederation did not set us on a course of reconciliation. Quite the contrary.

By contrast, and in an effort to correct the past, patriation was accompanied by a clear promise to Indigenous Peoples that moving forward, things would be different. It was a promise for the recognition of rights and reconciliation between Indigenous Peoples and the Crown. It is important to remember, though, that section 35 was not without its own controversy. Many Indigenous Peoples were skeptical of what was intended and whether the Crown could be trusted in this effort – in particular during the constitutional conferences that followed which were intended to spell out the right of self-government. Even in 1982 I think it is fair to say that the broader public did not have a strong appreciation of the legacy of colonialism that continued to exist in relation to Indigenous Peoples – including residential schools and the Indian Act, something that I believe today has changed somewhat and is supported by the release of the report of the Truth and Reconciliation Commission. The original vision at patriation, that the political conferences would chart the course for the implementation of section 35, never truly moved forward. This meant Indigenous Peoples had to take to the courts to force the implementation of section 35, and the courts responded, through hundreds of cases that have affirmed the importance, meaning, and strength of section 35 rights.

But what I have just described is also part of the challenge that we must now rise to. Instead of building relations based on recognition, the Crown has put Indigenous Peoples to the test of "proving" their rights through long and expensive litigation. Similarly, Canada often has adopted approaches to negotiations that do not engage the common work of implementing and protecting Indigenous Rights but rather is focused on trying to limit them.

In my opinion, the promise of section 35 is not one that lends itself to fulfillment through the courts or through protracted conflict. Reconciliation and adversarialism do not align. The promise of section 35 can be fulfilled only through proper and respectful nation-to-nation relationships. It is a promise that can be fulfilled only through political leadership and by the Crown and Indigenous Peoples making the hard choices to move out of past patterns of relations that do not work. We need to build the trust necessary to move from conflict to collaboration and to chart a course to a new and transformative future that addresses inequalities and injustices through recognition and reconciliation.

So, we all have hard work to do. First Nations, Inuit, and Métis Nations must come prepared to rebuild their nations and to assume the responsibilities that come from self-determination and self-government. Some are ready, willing, and able today. Some will require more time. In turn, Canada must do its part to support Indigenous Nations in this rebuilding work. Canada must confront the history of colonization and the denial of Indigenous Peoples and their rights, legacies of which we continue to be surrounded by today. Canada must review its laws and its policies to ensure that they align with a recognition-of-rights approach.

After too long, I am pleased to say that Canada is now undertaking this work. Last month, the Prime Minister struck a Working Group of Ministers on the Review of Laws and Policies Related to Indigenous Peoples. He appointed me chair of this working group. Its mandate is nothing short of transformative: it is to decolonize our federal laws and policies and to ensure that a recognition-of-rights approach is reflected in all aspects of Canada's relationship with Indigenous Peoples. No small task.

Yes, the task ahead will not be easy. Some aspects of our review will invite dissent. But every aspect of our work will be guided by the promise of section 35 and the direction from the courts, by Canada's unqualified support for the United Nations Declaration on the Rights of Indigenous Peoples, and by our government's commitment to implementing the Truth and Reconciliation Commission's Calls to Action. We will revisit the recommendations of the Royal Commission on Aboriginal Peoples.

In closing, let me say this: in many respects, the Charter and section 35 are closely aligned. Both constitutionally affirm the recognition of rights and both require a shift from the judicial leadership of the past thirty-five years to political leadership over the next thirty-five years and beyond. That said, I think we have made more political progress with respect to implementing the Charter than we have in implementing section 35.

Whether it is with respect to the Charter or section 35, political leadership requires, as a constant reminder, the ringing words of Prime Minister Pierre Trudeau during the Proclamation Ceremony of April 17, thirty-five years ago, when he said: "Let us celebrate the renewal and patriation of our Constitution; but let us put our faith, first and foremost, in the people of Canada who will breathe life into it." And as we begin to write the next chapter in our great country's story, there is much to be optimistic about – that we will, indeed, continue to collectively breathe life into our Constitution and in so doing set the standard for the globe in terms of freedoms and rights and the protection of equality for all.

Implementing UNDRIP

Address to the "Symposium on Implementing the UN Declaration
on the Rights of Indigenous Peoples:
Priorities, Partnerships, and Next Steps," November 20, 2017

The UN Declaration was completed in 2007 after years of diligent work. A decade has now passed. After years of reservations and qualifications by the previous government, I was very proud that our government fully and unequivocally endorsed the UN Declaration in May 2016.

The endorsement of the UN Declaration was reaching the starting line, not the finishing line. What this means today, in 2017, is that we are beyond old debates about "what" the minimum standards for the survival, dignity and well-being of Indigenous Peoples should be. The work of this moment in history is to take action and show "how" these minimum standards will be given life in tangible ways.

To say it another way, the time for talk and debate about the UN Declaration is over. The time for action implementing it in Canada is now.

Over the past two years, our government has taken many steps on the path of implementation. We are changing how the government engages and works with Indigenous Peoples, including initial shifts in negotiation, implementation, and litigation approaches. There have been specific initiatives around Indigenous languages, impact assessment, and fisheries, as well as new social investments, and the formation of new processes such as the Working Group of Ministers on the Review of Laws and Policies Related to Indigenous Peoples.

With the direction and leadership of Prime Minister Trudeau, our government will also support Bill C-262. This bill acknowledges the application of the UN Declaration in Canada and calls for the alignment of the laws of Canada with the UN Declaration. However, this step alone will not accomplish the full implementation of UNDRIP. A comprehensive approach, one that our government is committed to, will require other appropriate measures, including legislative measures, through the development of a recognition-of-rights framework. While a lot of positive steps have been taken, and Bill C-262 builds on those, we have far more work to do to effect reconciliation, implement the UN Declaration, and establish relations based on the recognition of Indigenous Rights.

To understand what this work involves, let me share with you my own definition of what reconciliation means. In my view, "reconciliation" means confronting and ending the legacy of colonialism in Canada and replacing it with a future built on Indigenous self-determination. Colonialism and Indigenous self-determination and self-government are antithetical to each other. To reach a future where self-determination and self-government are fully respected, it means we will have to remove the structures and restrictions of colonialism and embrace and encourage a reality where Nations are reconstituting, rebuilding, and thriving.

This definition of reconciliation is reflected at the core of the UN Declaration. Article 3 and Article 4 state: "Indigenous peoples have the right to self-determination. By virtue of that right, they freely determine their political status and freely pursue their economic, social and cultural development," and "Indigenous peoples, in exercising their right to self-determination, have the right to autonomy or self-government in matters relating to their internal and local affairs, as well as ways and means for financing their autonomous functions." Throughout the UN Declaration, we see the affirmation of the rights and roles of Indigenous Peoples in defining their structures; governing their lands and resources; educating their children and youth; transmitting their knowledge, language, and culture; and living their way of life.

I also define reconciliation in this way because it is personal to me and based on my own experience and learning. Being born and raised as an Indigenous woman in this country has meant – like First Nations, Métis,

and Inuit peoples across this country – that I was born into a colonial reality. I observed and experienced what the administration of my community
and Nation under the Indian Act has meant and the disempowerment and
harms it has perpetuated. This has included poverty and marginalization,
as well as the division of my people – the Kwakwaka'wakw people on the
west coast of Canada – into many bands and groupings, and interference
with our laws and governing structures.

At the same time, under the guidance of my grandmother, parents, and
family, I saw the resilience and strength of Indigenous Peoples striving
for self-determination. In the work of carrying forward our culture, laws,
identity, governing structures, roles, and responsibilities – my people, like
Indigenous Peoples across the country, have responded to colonialism
through efforts at self-determination and rebuilding their governments.
Ending the colonial structures that impeded that self-determination was the
life's work of my grandmother and father and of countless Indigenous
leaders across the country who advocate for full inclusion of First Nations,
Métis, and Inuit peoples in Canada. Self-determination is at the heart of what
reconciliation and the implementation of the UN Declaration is about.

So what actions do government and Indigenous Peoples need to take to
make such a vision a reality?

On the part of government, we must come to grips with the undeniable
fact that our legislation, policies, and operational practices do not reflect
the recognition of Indigenous Peoples' laws, governments, and rights and
are not aligned with minimum standards set out in the Declaration. The
work before us is to reflect recognition and the minimum standards at the
heart of legislation and policy. Aligning federal laws with the UN Declaration, such as through C-262, is one part of this, but there are three other
foundations that need to be laid.

First, the standard of recognition of rights, including the right of self-
determination and the inherent right of self-government, must be entrenched as the basis for conduct by federal officials in decision making,
negotiations, and actions. It is by setting the standard of recognition that
proper relations can be built and truly cooperative work can unfold. Setting
the standard of recognition also means that the minimum standards of the
UN Declaration would have to be integrated and reflected in all aspects of

how federal officials approach and undertake their work. This is what the Declaration itself points to when it speaks of "co-operative measures having to be taken to achieve its ends."

Setting the standard of recognition would also be a major step in the fulfillment of the promise of section 35. We have been stuck in thirty-five years of litigation about whether rights exist, and what they mean, when we could and should have been spending thirty-five years cooperatively implementing the full box of section 35 rights based on their recognition. By entrenching the standard of recognition, we can finally get to that point.

A first step was taken by our government through the ten "Principles Respecting the Government of Canada's Relationship with Indigenous Peoples." For those of you who have not had an opportunity to review these principles, I would encourage you to do so. They demonstrate our government's commitment to recognition and address many of the issues that will be vital to achieving reconciliation, including treaty implementation, the honour of the Crown, "free, prior, and informed consent," and the recognition of rights. The next step has to be recognition principles and standards being binding in legislation and reflected in policies and practices.

Second, we must create mechanisms to help facilitate and support Indigenous self-determination and the inherent right of self-government, including transition out of the Indian Act. Indigenous Nations across the country are doing the work of advancing their visions and priorities for how they will govern their peoples, lands, and resources. This work, however, is hampered by the obstacles that existing federal laws and policies have created. Thankfully, this has been changing, but too slowly and not evenly. There have been successes, from sectoral governance agreements to modern treaties and land claims agreements.

Today, the typical pattern of Crown-Indigenous relations is that decades of negotiations are required for rights recognition and implementation. Alternatively, millions of dollars might be spent in treaty implementation and litigation, often with negotiations still being needed. This is true for Indigenous Governance Rights and Indigenous Rights more broadly. This denial and delay has to stop, as we need to ensure that the space is created for all Indigenous Peoples to succeed.

We have to shift to a context that embraces the many diverse paths that Indigenous Peoples may choose to follow and where Indigenous Nations who are ready and willing have the supports in place to move towards self-government. There also needs to be positive obligations on the federal government to respond to the visions and priorities that Indigenous Nations set as self-determining peoples. Canada must create the legislative and policy space so that the directions Indigenous Peoples determine for themselves can become their reality.

Third, for generations, justifiable mistrust has built up in the Crown-Indigenous relationship. Governments have often not followed through on promises made and understandings reached, including historic treaties. Further, the struggle to implement modern treaties and land claims agreements and the acceleration in the use of the courts in recent decades illustrate the ongoing impacts of this mistrust. Of course, the failure to uphold such agreements and understandings is wholly inconsistent with the Declaration and the standards set out in Article 37 [which states that "Indigenous peoples have the right to the recognition, observance and enforcement of treaties, agreements and other constructive arrangements concluded with States or their successors ..."]. Indigenous Peoples have a right to see such understandings recognized and respected.

We have to continue to build a climate and culture where commitments are followed through and actions and words are aligned. This is something that is being worked on across government. For example, at the Department of Justice, we are actively working to align our decision making and approaches to litigation with the recognition of rights and the imperative of reconciliation. In doing this work, we will also advance a shift from conflict and litigation to cooperation as the norm of our relations. This requires new mechanisms for accountability and new opportunities for the federal government and Indigenous Peoples to collaboratively resolve disputes that arise on the path of recognition and implementation of their rights.

In addition to these three actions, there is vitally important work Indigenous Peoples must define and undertake for themselves. Self-determination means that Indigenous Peoples are setting their own priorities, defining and refining their visions of governance now and into the future, and working to continue to build the capacity to make those a reality. No Crown government – or anyone else – can lead or do this work.

This means hard questions have to be asked and answered by Indigenous Peoples. This is not easy – and many of the answers will require challenging common assumptions and rejecting things that are currently taken for granted. Some of these questions include the following:

- How will you organize your government into the future?
- What processes and structures will you use to confirm your laws?
- What mechanisms will be used to ensure the legitimacy of your governments and the participation and support of your members?
- What are the ways in which you foresee interacting with Crown governments in making decisions and implementing your laws and policies?
- What are the capacities that need to be built to give life to or propel this vision of government?
- How will the UN Declaration be reflected in the structures, modes of operation, and standards that guide your current or future governance?

It also means, particularly for First Nations, that the divisions caused by the imposition of the Indian Act and the imposition of band councils as an impoverished notion of government have to be addressed. Part of the work of self-determination is figuring out how each traditional rights-bearing collective will work and govern together in protecting their culture, way of life, lands, resources, and society.

Reconstituting as peoples and Nations and rebuilding governments go hand in hand in ending colonization and meeting the promise held in the UN Declaration and section 35 of our Constitution. We are in a moment of transition – with vast work before us to implement the UN Declaration and move beyond our colonial reality. There is no road map to follow. If we are doing our work in implementing the UN Declaration properly, we will be setting an example that people across the globe will look towards. I think this is one of the most exciting moments in the history of this country. It is a moment of fulfilling promises. Through this transformative work, a new future will be possible for generations to come.

Governance in the
Post-Indian Act World

"

Indian Act government is not self-government.

It is an impoverished notion of government

where the Chief and council are, for the most part,

glorified Indian Agents delivering federal programs

and services on behalf of Canada.

"

Toppling the Indian Act Tree

Address to the First Nations–Crown Gathering, January 24, 2012

Our people are in a profound period of transition and of Nation building or rebuilding. We are, in fact, making economic progress. It may not be widely known but a significant economic transformation has already begun. The economists at TD, with the support of the Canadian Council for Aboriginal Business, estimate that the combined income of Aboriginal households, business, and government sectors reached $24 billion in 2011, double the $12 billion tally recorded in 2001. By 2016, they estimate this overall economic pie could eclipse $32 billion – or roughly 50 percent above last year's estimate. If achieved, the total Aboriginal income would be greater than the GDP of Newfoundland and Prince Edward Island combined. This is good news. We are trending in the right direction.

But truth be told, we can and must do much more. Any optimism and progress are overshadowed by the deplorable conditions faced in many of our Nations – particularly in the North – where such encouraging growth numbers mean nothing in the face of crippling poverty and desperation. This is totally unacceptable. We need to collectively find ways to ensure no Nation is left out or behind and that all our peoples are supported. Strengthening First Nation economies will certainly help. It will also strengthen the Canadian economy and provide opportunities for not only our people but also for other Canadians.

Canada is emerging out of one of the worst global economic crises in modern history but faring better than most industrialized economies. When the crisis began and governments implemented "economic stimulus" programs, many of our Chiefs reflected that their Nations' economies had been in a state of crisis for years and were definitely in need of stimulus. One of the biggest stimuluses for us must be governance reform. Societies that govern well simply do better economically, socially, and politically than those that do not. Good governance increases a society's chance of meeting the needs of its peoples and developing sustainable long-term economic development.

Within Canada, the structure and institutions of non-Aboriginal government are well established within a sound legal framework. Today, most Canadians just take for granted the way their economy works and the legal and political framework that supports it.

Contrast that to the governments of the people whom the Chiefs in this room represent. While historically we were, of course, self-governing, more recently we have been under federal administrative authority and our peoples and our lands and consequently our economies governed separate and apart from non-Aboriginal Canada in accordance with the Indian Act – neither an appropriate governance framework for First Nations People nor for any people, for that matter.

During the colonial period, band government was based on models developed by the federal government to deliver federal programs and services. The powers of our governments were very limited. The effects on us were unfortunate. The Indian Act system promoted an impoverished concept of government. "Government" for us became little more than managing programs and distributing limited resources. The concept that government should be about making laws, resolving disputes, and generating the means to pursue a collective vision was smothered under the need for federal programs and services and the fact that the local "band office" was the instrument to deliver them. This is not self-government. This is not a system that supports strong economies and can provide a sound investment climate.

Thankfully, this is changing. And why is this changing? Because there are First Nations leaders who have supported and led both sectoral and comprehensive self-government initiatives to replace governance under the Indian Act, to create the legal and administrative framework of self-government that other Canadians take for granted and to establish a sound investment climate. This includes the raising of local revenues and financial management, the building of public infrastructure and facilities and the raising of capital, and the management of land and resources and community planning.

Today, there is now a general consensus that supporting First Nations' developing strong and appropriate governance – or self-government – is simply the right thing to do. And why is it the right thing to do? Because Canada's economy and First Nations, and our collective futures, are all intertwined. If we want to unlock our economic potential, it is needed.

Ironically, while we all may now agree that we need to move away from the Indian Act towards self-government, I do not need to tell anyone in this room what a challenge this has become. The reality of our post-colonial transition is that short of a court saying we have rights over land and the right to govern ourselves, our people have to vote to remove Canada from its paternalistic role in our lives. This is because under the Indian Act, we are still wards of the state. Consequently, Canada has a fiduciary responsibility to our people and cannot simply legislate the Indian Act away in favour of recognizing self-government until our people vote in favour that it is okay to do so – legally challenging, politically perverse but nevertheless true.

No other segment of Canadian society has had to decolonize and then go through this process to establish basic structures of governance to create the tools for economic and social development. However, today we have the tools – section 35 (full box) and the United Nations Declaration on the Rights of Indigenous Peoples (minimum standards for engagement with our people). The challenge now is to translate the promise of section 35 and the UNDRIP into practical benefits on the ground in our communities.

While our leaders have advocated and continue to advocate for change back home on reserve, many of our people are afraid and reluctant to vote "yes" to self-government. Given the colonial legacy and the impoverished concept of governance under the Indian Act, they simply do not trust their existing "band" government nor, if we are being frank, your government, for that matter. This is now one of our biggest challenges.

For change to occur each of our communities must go through our own processes of empowerment and local transformation, through healing, rebuilding, capacity development – call it what you may. Our colonial period must officially end. As this process of decolonization continues to unfold, we all have a responsibility to support what is essentially basic community development work. We must all not add fuel to the fire by trying to circumvent this process.

While we are making progress and while, as you said today, Mr. Prime Minister, your government is making a down payment on our long-term goal of self-government, we must be mindful that it is a down payment on the "right house," one where we make choices collectively, where our Nations lead the change to uproot the Indian Act tree and knock it over, leading to full self-government, not a down payment where your government rebuilds our governance for us through federally imposed initiatives.

So, with all due respect, Mr. Prime Minister, on this point we must ask that you please rethink your government's approach set out in a number of recent bills introduced or proposed affecting our peoples, which seek to tinker around the edges of the Indian Act in a piecemeal way, with federally imposed solutions to our issues and in advance of our Nations having first had the opportunity to address core governance reform. Unfortunately, this attempt to legislate aspects of self-governance for us is, to put it bluntly, and again I say this with all due respect, an exercise in neocolonialism and, as history has shown, will not work, however well intentioned. The approach is fraught with legal and political problems at many levels. This process of change has to be led by our people to be legitimate.

There is still a need, however, for federal legislation that is First Nations–led, legislation developed jointly with our Nations. Not least we need governance recognition legislation, so that when a Nation is ready, willing, and able there is an efficient mechanism so it can move away from the Indian Act and establish its core institutions of governance without the federal government acting as gatekeeper and without interminable negotiations that take years to conclude. This is the foundational work we need to undertake and reconfirm determining citizenship in our Nations, how we select our governing bodies, how we make laws, and how our governments are accountable to our people. This is really the starting point to all other governance reform, including creating the legal and administrative framework to support economic development.

Recognition legislation to achieve this goal is not a new idea but perhaps finally an idea whose time has come. It was recommended by the Penner Committee on Self-Government. It was recommended by the Royal Commission. It has been supported by our Chiefs. Frankly, it just makes good sense. This will get at the roots of the Indian Act tree – we need core governance reform. When we do, the Indian Act tree will topple over. No gaping hole, Mr. Prime Minister, but strong and self-determining First Nations.

However, to move our governance agenda forward, it will take leadership, by you and by us. We cannot simply say it is too difficult or too big, if we are truly serious about economic and social development and the advancement of our peoples. It will also take financial resources, resources that can come from our Nations having fair access to our lands and resources and revenue sharing with the provinces. There will also need to be new investments made by your government. We know your government rejected the Kelowna Accord, but it is that level of investment that is needed – well-planned out and tied to a solid vision of a post-Indian Act world, investments that will ensure quality education and provide for improved individual health. In fact, what we really need is a new fiscal relationship and a commitment to deal with issues such as own-source revenue. We need to ensure our Nations have the resources to provide comparable level of services as other Canadians expect and receive.

In conclusion, our peoples are beginning to take back control of our lives. Where governance reform has been successful, whether through sectoral or comprehensive initiatives, economic opportunity has followed. I, for one, like many of my colleagues, am excited about our opportunities. We have the solutions – and we need to build on our success. But let us not forget, unlocking the economic potential is not the end in itself but is, rather, a means to an end, that end being healthier and more prosperous First Nations communities, with our people enjoying a better quality of life with practising and thriving cultures. We must never lose sight of the objective.

And finally, Mr. Prime Minister, this Gathering provides you with an opportunity to demonstrate that you are a true Canadian and committed to undertaking the necessary steps to support OUR Nations along their journey. Our people are watching. Canadians are watching. After Attawapiskat, the world is watching. Canada's reputation – our reputation as a country of caring and compassionate peoples and as a leader internationally – is at stake.

We need direct leadership from you to smash the status quo and ensure that Aboriginal People in this country are truly engaged in, and benefitting from, the economy as much as anyone else.

Our people and all Canadians expect you and your government to do the right thing.

First Nations Jurisdiction over Citizenship

Remarks to the Senate Standing Committee on Human Rights, Bill C-3: Gender Equity in Indian Registration Act, December 6, 2010

First Nations are truly in an exciting period of Nation building or rebuilding and moving away from governance under the Indian Act. We are in the process of establishing a new relationship with Canada, one that is based on the implementation of our rights protected under section 35 of the Canadian Constitution and must now respect the principles and standards set out in the United Nations Declaration on Indigenous Peoples, as recently endorsed by Canada. I am confident our peoples have a bright future within Confederation.

There is, however, considerable work ahead of us, and not everyone shares the same optimism that I do. The legacy of the Indian Act is significant and creates many challenges for all of us in making real progress and moving forward. It is not easy to shed well over a hundred years of paternalism and wardship and move to meaningful self-determination.

It is in this context that I ask you to consider Bill C-3 and the challenge of reconciling the question of who is entitled to be registered as an "Indian" under the Indian Act and the broader question of who is entitled to be citizens of our Nations, a challenge that both lawmakers for Canada, such as yourselves, and lawmakers in our own Nations must now address. This is no easy task, as evidenced by the political conversation and the controversy that has already surrounded Bill C-3.

The current confusion and debate between citizenship and Indian status has its origins in how, since the mid-1850s, Canada has tried to control our identity by defining who is legally an "Indian." Initially, the definition of "Indian" was quite broad and more reflective of how we saw ourselves. The first "legal" definition of who was an Indian included any person either of Indian birth or blood, reputed to belong to a particular group of Indians, married to an Indian, or adopted into an Indian family. This definition became more and more restrictive, in an effort to enfranchise our peoples and to assimilate them into Canadian culture, and since 1869 these narrow definitions specifically targeted First Nations women.

Leadership made objections to these restrictions, specifically the loss of legal status to women who married non-Native men. However, the government did not respond to those objections. Since then, this ongoing discrimination has had numerous, adverse effects on our Nations, our communities, and our families.

The 1985 Bill C-31 amendments to the Indian Act took steps to address this discrimination but at the same time created new discrimination and divisions in the introduction of differing categories of registrants and application of the law. The *McIvor* (2009) case sought to deal with these issues and now, with Bill C-3, we have the opportunity to correct the ongoing discrimination.

Therefore, and notwithstanding the broader question around Nation building, let me state – unequivocally – that the Assembly of First Nations and First Nations leadership support removing all discrimination against our peoples that exists in legislation. Any discrimination is not acceptable. This position was affirmed by AFN resolution prior to the introduction of Bill C-3, and at our Annual General Assembly in Winnipeg in July the Chiefs-in-Assembly reaffirmed their collective support to remove all discrimination.

When Bill C-3 was eventually introduced in March of this year, I publicly welcomed the introduction of the bill but, along with other leaders, called on the government to address the ongoing discrimination in the Indian Act that was not resolved in the bill as well as address the broader issues of First Nations jurisdiction. Bill C-3, to be clear, should have gone further in addressing the broader discrimination under the Indian Act. Amendments were proposed and made at the committee stage. Unfortunately, these amendments were ruled beyond the scope of the bill by the speaker and disallowed. Because these amendments were not made, Sharon McIvor has not only called for rejecting this legislation, she has moved to file a complaint with the United Nations Human Rights Committee.

Should the Senate see fit to reconsider the proposed amendments to Bill C-3 and recommend again their approval to the House, the AFN would, of course, be supportive. However, caution should be exercised that the bill is not lost and we do not lose the opportunity to address the most egregious discrimination in accordance with the direction of the court.

While I recognize that Bill C-3 is not a complete solution to rectifying discrimination under the Indian Act, in the interests of those who will be directly affected by this bill, including persons who may be denied registration in BC, the bill, with or without amendments, must proceed. Passage of the bill will address the specific discrimination addressed by the BC Court of Appeal and will also ensure the uninterrupted and continued registration of all persons in BC who are currently entitled to registration under section 6(1)(a) and 6(1)(c) of the Indian Act. The court has given until January 31 to make the necessary amendments.

If, as it now seems likely, this imperfect bill will become law, it is also critically important that there are adequate resources provided to First Nations to address the increased numbers of registrants. This is particularly important where First Nations are providing programs and services on behalf of Canada in their communities and where already stretched resources will be stretched even more because of the new registrants. This was the experience after Bill C-31 was passed in 1985. Resource implications will be felt most acutely at the community level but will also have impacts for other federal programs provided directly to individuals, such as Non-Insured Health Benefits.

I now want to turn to the broader question of citizenship. Since the original trial decision in *McIvor* (2007), I have heard from a number of First Nations People, both men and women, who are genuinely excited about the prospect of becoming registered under the Indian Act as a result of the proposed amendments. At one level, this is about correcting discrimination, but at a more fundamental level it is about belonging and association with a group. While for policy-makers and administrators the issue of increasing members might be viewed simply in terms of budget pressures, service provision, and access to resources, at its core, however, this is about community, and this is powerful. Our people are our greatest resource.

In British Columbia, as in other parts of the country, our Nations are developing our own models of citizenship. The Nation decides who is a part of that Nation, who is a citizen, notwithstanding the legacy of the Indian Act and memberships. In the context of modern claims, the determination of citizenship is a fundamental conversation that results in the collective setting the rules and the individual electing to be a citizen or not. Citizens are beneficiaries of treaties and can participate in the political institutions created through the treaty or agreement but – and more importantly for the collective – in exchange are subject to the obligations of citizenship.

In announcing the proposed amendments to the Indian Act, then Minister Strahl also announced an exploratory process centred on registration, membership, and citizenship issues. While this announcement was met favourably, I am very disappointed that Canada has not made any progress on this process and is insisting that it be contingent on the passage of C-3. With the recent endorsement of the United Nations Declaration on the Rights of Indigenous Peoples, Canada needs to move forward on this process in good faith, with clear commitment to meaningful outcomes. A discussion of citizenship within the broad context of Nation building would be evidence of a fundamental shift in the relationship between our Nations and the Crown, which is consistent with the spirit and intent of the historic treaties and necessary to conclude modern land claims arrangements with Nations that enjoy unextinguished Aboriginal Title and Rights. It reflects the beginning of a healthier and more mature relationship between our peoples and the Crown, not only with respect to the determination of citizenship outside of the Indian Act, but also to govern through our own institutions of government with appropriate jurisdiction and authority outside of the Indian Act.

There are many opportunities for First Nations in this country, but there are necessary prerequisites before our Nations will fully realize these opportunities. First and foremost, there is a need for appropriate governance, which includes, of course, the determination of citizenship. There is also a need for fair access to lands and resources so our First Nations economies are viable, with adequate own-source revenue generation, the power to support critical aspects of our governance, and the provision of programs and services. In addition to appropriate governance and lands and resource settlements, we, of course, need well-educated and healthy citizens. Our citizens, perhaps more than any other Canadians, are required to participate in decision making around our own very existence and future.

In closing, long-term solutions do not lie in further tinkering with the Indian Act. Our Nations have an inherent right to determine who is and who is not a citizen of our Nation in accordance with our own laws, customs, and traditions. This is fundamental to self-governance. The real and ultimate solution to addressing ongoing discrimination in the Indian Act lies with full recognition of First Nations jurisdiction over our own citizenship. The contribution that will be made by our full citizenry, when legally recognized through appropriate citizenship processes and in part supported by interim legislation such as Bill C-3, will be profound. Finally, Parliament is in a unique position to work in partnership with First Nations to undertake a comprehensive review of the Indian Act, its related policies and regulations, and their intrusion into First Nations jurisdiction and to put forward mechanisms for recognition and staged and supported implementation of First Nations jurisdiction.

Holding and Managing Our Lands

Adapted from address to Insight: Aboriginal Land Resource
Management Forum, January 31, 2012

First Nations are in a period of transition. We are building, rebuilding, our Nations. We are seeking fair access to land and resources beyond our small reserves. We are looking to share in both the decision making with respect to our Traditional Lands and to benefit from those lands (where we agree with the proposed land use) as well as to govern our existing reserve lands or settlement lands. Here, I would like to focus on the management of our existing reserves or settlement lands and our success at moving away from governance under the Indian Act. We are asking ourselves some very fundamental questions: How is our land to be held? How are interests in land created? Who can hold interests in land? How are we going to govern and administer our lands?

In fact, it is not just our Nations that are looking at this subject – the Aboriginal Affairs House of Commons Committee is also proposing to study what it calls "Land Use Modernization." However, let us not forget that jurisdiction and control over land is only one aspect of governance. It cannot be isolated from the much broader question of how our governments will ultimately be re-established post-Indian Act and the substantial challenges of moving beyond. The systems of land tenure and governance structures our Nations create will be guided by the policy objectives of our governments, reflecting the will of our peoples based on our respective cultures and traditions.

Prior to colonization, historically, our Nations were, of course, self-governing, operating within our tribal structures. Each of our Nations had ways in which access to lands and resources were controlled. In my own Tribe, we had, and still have, a hereditary governing system where names are transferred from generation to generation through the successions of Chiefs, each with responsibilities for certain geographical areas. This land tenure system is conducted through our Potlatch. For many years, this traditional system of government was illegal under federal law. As our peoples were moved onto reserves, the Indian Act created a different system of land tenure for the reserves that essentially made us tenants on our own lands under the wardship of the Crown, with limited or no jurisdiction. As government and laws evolved generally in Canada, our people were not allowed to govern ourselves and therefore were not able to adapt. As a result of this system, the court in *Musqueam Indian Band v Glass* (2000) concluded that the land management provisions of the Indian Act had had a devaluing effect on Musqueam Reserve land by 50 percent to that of similar adjacent nonreserve lands.

Anyone who has worked under the Indian Act system of land management is aware that First Nations or their citizens cannot operate at the speed of business and either lose economic development opportunities or cannot maximize their return because of the way that Act operates, where decision making is in the hands of risk-averse bureaucrats or Department of Justice lawyers or where there are inevitable hurdles to overcome in trying to use land as security (although, it can be said that some have become quite good at making a round peg fit into a square hole, getting around the Indian Act in the absence of there being a viable mechanism available to a First Nation for getting out from under it). In addition to the obvious issues of taking security and registering interests in lands, the antiquated Indian Act system has created a legacy of other major issues on our lands, such as incomplete survey boundaries, environmental contamination, or establishing conflicting property interests to local or customary land tenure practices. These issues and others have been left to fester for decades and only serve to impede a community's ability to implement responsive and sustainable land-use planning and growth and to address community priorities.

In short, there is one matter I think that we can all agree on: the Indian Act is not an appropriate system of government, including land management. There is a need for reform where it has not already been achieved.

So why has it been so hard to move beyond the Indian Act? Why, in some political circles, is there a reluctance to move beyond the Indian Act? And why have people been forced to fit that round peg into a square hole, a reality that we need to understand in order to make progress? While aspects of the Indian Act with respect to the management of lands are abhorrent to us and have held us back, ironically, other aspects are actually consistent with the current policy objectives of many of our people. This needs to be considered in any replacement to the Indian Act. On the one hand, the Indian Act has imposed colonial concepts of government, membership, and management of lands that have had negative effects on our people, while, on the other hand, protections that respect the communal nature and ultimate inalienability of reserve lands are still important to many of us.

Over the past twenty years, great strides have been made in many communities to move beyond the Indian Act. Every community that has begun the process of decolonization with respect to land management has addressed the question of appropriate governance over lands and types of land tenure on reserve. They have each considered how land is to be held, how private interests in land are to be created and registered, and how local decisions about land use are made and authorized. We can learn a lot from their valuable experiences. Interestingly, all have included some aspect of collective ownership and control while all have also created some form of private interests in land with the registration of those interests, where interests are recorded in priority to one another.

For example, in 2009, my own community, We Wai Kai, voted in favour of our own land code under the Framework Agreement on First Nation Land Management, and we are establishing a system of land tenures and laws relating to land management. Let me give you one example of what this means for our citizens, including myself. Before our land code came into effect, the house where my husband and I now live was owned by

Canada, administered by the Chief and council, and governed under the Indian Act. When I purchased that house from the previous occupier, another band member, in reality that person had no legal interest under the Indian Act to sell the house to me, and there was no way to register my interest save for the letter we filed in a filing cabinet kept in our band office. Today, after the land code, my once informal or extralegal interest in my house is now legally recognized and registerable in the First Nations Land Registry system. If I ever want to sell it, I will be able to do so without the approval of Chief and council or the involvement of Canada. Many of our Nations have informal, customary, or extralegal, however you want to call them, land interests on their reserves. In fact, this is the norm. These interests can be legalized through a First Nation taking control over land management.

Looking at another example I am personally familiar with, my family has property in North Vancouver on the Tsleil-Waututh Reserve. Here, we also have a private interest in land. In this case, a ninety-nine-year prepaid lease that is also registered in the First Nations Land Registry. Tsleil-Waututh also has a land code in place and has full authority over the management of their lands. Today, in fact, there is a continuum of options for First Nations, should they wish to take on the challenge of land management or governance. These range from

- delegated authority under the Indian Act, where the First Nation becomes the agent of the minister
- sectoral self-government, including where the First Nation asserts its own decision making over reserve lands and resources under the Framework Agreement on First Nation Land Management and opts out of the land administration provisions of the Indian Act (approximately 25 percent of bands) and the First Nations Commercial and Industrial Development Act, which allows First Nations to establish fee simple on some or all of their reserve lands for economic development purposes and register them provincially (being led by Squamish First Nation)
- comprehensive self-government (like Westbank First Nation) or under modern treaties such as with Tsawwassen, Maa-nulth, and Nisga'a.

In some of these examples, land is held under section 91(24) of the Constitution Act, and in other cases under section 92 and/or section 35.

The Framework Agreement on First Nation Land Management was the first time in Canadian history that First Nations from across the country came together as a group to develop, negotiate, and sign a government-to-government arrangement with Canada with respect to land management. In 1992, there were fourteen Chiefs from across Canada searching for a way to take back control of their reserve lands and resources. In 1996, they negotiated and signed the Framework Agreement with Canada. In 1999, Parliament passed the First Nations Land Management Act, ratifying Canada's commitment to the Framework Agreement.

On January 1, 2000, day one of the new millennium, three First Nations began operating under their own land codes and resumed jurisdiction over their reserve lands and resources, no longer held back by the paternalistic Indian Act. Today, fifty-eight First Nations are signatories to the Framework Agreement, and thirty-seven First Nations now have ratified their land codes. A few days ago, in Ottawa, Minister Duncan announced a further eighteen additional signatories, beginning in April 2012. Together, the seventy-six signatory First Nations represent 12 percent of all First Nations in Canada. Sixty-five other First Nations are currently on a "waiting list" to be added as signatories. Hopefully, the wait will not be too long.

First Nations are responding to economic development opportunities at the speed of business, as the following statistics indicate:

- $53 million investment from member-owned businesses
- $100 million investment from third-party businesses
- more than two thousand employment opportunities for band members
- more than ten thousand employment opportunities for nonmembers, pumping hundreds of millions of dollars into local economies
- administration costs per land transaction reduced to an average of $500 by First Nations, compared to Canada's cost of more than $2,500.

In my opinion, the Framework Agreement has been a success because it was developed and led by First Nations, not Canada, and continues to be led by First Nations.

For First Nations government to succeed, whether sectoral or compre-hensive, the work must be developed by our people. It must be legitimate. Developing your own land code is empowering. Further, many First Nations have opted into the Framework Agreement because it maintains reserve lands and in particular the collective ownership of the reserves for the use and benefit of "Indians." This is important for many First Nations. The lands cannot be surrendered and sold because they must be protected for future generations. Fee simple title is not allowed. This does not mean that there are no private interests in land permitted – quite the contrary. What it does mean, though, is that fee simple interests that can be alienated or sold to noncitizens are not permitted. Finally, I believe the main reason that First Nations have opted into the framework is that it provides com-prehensive land-management jurisdiction where full decision making and control is the responsibility of the community, not Canada.

Moving along the continuum of governance options, some Nations have addressed lands and land management as part of comprehensive governance arrangements. Tsawwassen, for example, has negotiated their land manage-ment arrangements in the context of a modern treaty. Through the treaty arrangements, Tsawwassen opted to take their lands in fee simple, and they have full land management authority that is, unlike the Framework Agreement, constitutionally protected. Interestingly, they have, however, put restric-tions on how the collective fee simple interests can be alienated so that only Tsawwassen or Tsawwassen members can hold the fee simple. Westbank First Nation, under its self-government model (which was negotiated outside of the BC treaty-making process bilaterally with Canada) also restricts the hold-ing of certificates of possession (which are interests in land treated like fee simple under Westbank's Constitution) to members of Westbank First Nation.

In both the Tsawwassen and Westbank examples of land management under self-government, marketable private interests in land can be created through leaseholds to any person. Significantly, this right has been balanced with the policy decision to maintain the collective interests of the commun-ity. Both at Westbank and Tsawwassen, land prices for all types of interests have been increasing with growing real estate markets – in fact, they have skyrocketed. At Westbank, the ability to get "title" insurance on long-term leases has also enhanced land values.

Part of the reason for restricting private interests is that many urban First Nations such as Westbank and Tsawwassen have a land base that is relatively small in terms of area but potentially, when the Indian Act is removed, high in terms of value. Here, the issue is not just about the types of interest in land that are created but about the extent of the underlying jurisdiction of the First Nation and the ability to control the access to assets once the restrictions of the Indian Act have been removed.

The fear at both Westbank and Tsawwassen, as I understand it, was that economic pressures could result in a large redistribution of unrestricted fee simple property from the poor to the rich and potentially to non-Aboriginal people, which could create a whole host of new social challenges and which could be counterproductive to Nation building. What is the point of trying to build a Nation and a community if everybody has left – whether because they wanted to or had to for market reasons? At Tsawwassen and Westbank, and in every other community that has gone through a community process to address these issues and move beyond the Indian Act, this has been a concern. The cultural attachment of the citizens in these communities to their lands precludes any option that puts the underlying fee simple ownership at risk and, if it does so, only to a limited extent. Here, a lesson learned is that while economic development is important, it is not the end objective but rather a means to an end – strong and healthy communities.

The question today, as it has been in the past, is this: What are the appropriate ways to create private interests in land on our reserves, and how best to register those interests while balancing the need for economic development with the policy considerations of preserving community? In fact, any band today under the Indian Act could have a vote to ultimately surrender their reserve lands and become incorporated within the provincial governing structures and raise title. What is telling is that no community has ever done this, and where they have raised title after treaty and actually done so using provincial institutions, they have been very careful to ensure that the full jurisdiction required to govern those lands is in place first and that the only party who can benefit to the fullest extent of that title once raised is the members of the community or the community as a whole through their government.

The Nisga'a, through the Nisga'a Landholding Transition Act, provides another model of how, under its full jurisdiction over lands in accordance with its modern treaty, the Nation has been able to make independent decisions with respect to its types of land interests as it responds to local economic realities. The Nisga'a have provided for the full transferability of fee simple lands on a very limited basis – approximately 0.05 percent of their total land base – while limiting the transferability for the vast majority. With full jurisdiction over the management of lands, Nisga'a, along with the other communities that are already beyond the Indian Act, have not had to sacrifice the community's desires for the sake of economic development. Quite the contrary. Full or exclusive jurisdiction is a core component to not only creating a marketable system of land tenure but also ensuring that community concerns regarding the potential loss of ownership are also taken into consideration.

If we consider how the concept of Aboriginal Title has evolved through the courts, it is important to understand that the importance of the collective interest in land and the need to protect "community" is also now a legal requirement. The *Delgamuukw* decision (1997) provided judicial affirmation of Aboriginal Title by the country's highest court: the court said that Aboriginal Title existed before, and exists after, the assertion of sovereignty by colonial authority and, important for this discussion, is a collective right held by all members of a First Nation. It was made clear in *Delgamuukw* that lands held pursuant to Aboriginal Title cannot be used in a manner that is irreconcilable with the nature of the group's attachment to those lands. More recently, the *Tsilhqot'in* decision, in *William* (although only a trial decision, and we are currently waiting to hear from the BC Court of Appeal), confirmed that Aboriginal Title is held collectively by the members of a Nation and is distinct from the legal entity (political structure) that represents them. The court goes on to say that Indian bands, as creatures of a federal statute, are not necessarily the entity-holding title. We have to be mindful of what the court is saying when we consider lands and land management.

What I can say with confidence is that we can learn from our experiences and that we should not understate the importance of a community going through a process to determine its own land tenure system, considering a range of issues that include its historical systems of tenure and those tenures that may have existed extralegally to the Indian Act and others. Regardless of the legal debate of who has the right to govern, politically, if systems are to be supported and endorsed locally, the community development work is critical. First Nations need to know the options and the implications of their choices with regard to re-establishing governance, including land management, particularly at this time when there are so many options out there and perhaps new options being considered. As you are all aware, the BC Assembly of First Nations supports unequivocally the right of our Nations to determine their own future and choose their own options for land management.

At the BCAFN, we have developed *The Governance Toolkit: A Guide to Nation Building*, which includes a *Governance Report*, that looks at the options for First Nations governing under and beyond the Indian Act along a continuum. Chapter 3.19, "Land Management," provides more detail about the land management initiatives and the work of the First Nations I have discussed above, among others. A copy of the toolkit was sent to each First Nation and can be found on our website, along with links to many of the codes and laws our Nations are making.

While communities start to consider their post-Indian Act future, Canada will, to be sure, continue to enact or seek to enact legislation that addresses aspects of our governance. In some cases, this legislation may be led by our peoples. In other cases, it could be the result of court cases. In others, it may be led by policy direction from Aboriginal Affairs and Northern Development Canada or cabinet. Examples of federally led legislation currently making their way through Parliament include Bill C-27; the Accountability Act; and Bill S-2, the Family Homes on Reserves and Matrimonial Interests or Rights Act. There is also legislation proposed for drinking-water standards.

As the Regional Chief and as the holder of the National Assembly of First Nations portfolio for Nation building and First Nations governance, I will continue to remind Canada that these federal legislative initiatives must, if they do go ahead, only be seen as interim until communities rebuild, and they must be consistent with our broader Nation-building agenda. They are not a substitute for the end goal, which is re-establishing our Nations with appropriate governance and strong polities. It is important that our energies and our resources, limited as they are, are focused on decolonization in our communities and Nation building. The fact that many of our communities are not even having this conversation or even ready to move towards self-government should not be used as an excuse for avoiding the complex issues of decolonization in favour of further imposition of federal laws.

I would like to leave you with an idea that could impact land management. For some time now, an idea has been proposed for a Self-Government Recognition Act, which would facilitate communities moving beyond the Indian Act without the interminable negotiations with Canada and without Canada acting as a gatekeeper and where, I would argue, the energies and resources could be expended on community development work. We need an efficient mechanism for recognizing our nationhood, one consistent with the state of the common law and the United Nations Declaration on the Rights of Indigenous Peoples, to be put in place so that any First Nation or group of First Nations can move through the postcolonial door and get out from under the Indian Act and re-establish their core institutions of government by developing their own constitution and voting on it, a constitution setting out the rules for determining citizenship, how the governing body is selected, the law-enactment process, and perhaps even the rules governing the management of lands. In many respects, such foundational work is the cornerstone to other governance reform and is really, for many First Nations, the first step on the continuum of moving out from under the Indian Act.

In conclusion, our people have been consistent in the portrayal of our sacred relationship with our lands. Our Elders have taught us that our land, our culture, our languages, and our identity are all intertwined. It is not just the Indigenous Peoples' place in law that makes us unique. Life in our communities – on our lands and territories, among our families, our cultures, our languages, and our traditions – is a unique and precious gift, a respite from all that is everywhere else. While we want economic development, it should not be at the expense of our cultures and our peoples and our values. The benefits of taking back control of land management and creating private interests in our lands and developing property markets must be balanced with our collective interests. The preservation of our lands for future generations is a sacred, inalienable trust, carried forward by each generation. This has been our way, our tradition, since time immemorial. It is on these principles that leading court cases have been argued and won.

First Nations control and jurisdiction over lands and resources, whether exclusively on-reserve or settlement lands or shared over a broader Traditional Territory, is of critical importance, not only to the future prosperity of our peoples but also to the future prosperity of BC and Canada as a whole. So is overall governance reform. It has been said, and I know it remains true today, "The land belongs not only to people presently living, but also to past and future generations, who are considered to be as much a part of the tribal entity as the present generation." At the end of the day, any land management initiative that we advocate or support as First Nations leaders should have as its ultimate objective the improvement of the quality of life of our people with practising and thriving cultures. Anything less our people will no doubt reject.

On Accountability and Transparency

Presentation to the Standing Senate Committee on Aboriginal Peoples,
Bill C-27: First Nations Financial Transparency Act, March 5, 2013

I presented on Bill C-27: First Nations Financial Transparency Act before the Commons Standing Committee on October 17, 2012. Some minor changes have been made to the bill, but it is substantially in the same form as it was then. Our core concerns with the bill remain the same, both in terms of the substance and the process by which it was developed. I believe some of the changes made were an attempt to respond to concerns that the bill creates a different standard for First Nations than for other governments in Canada but, ironically, in making them, actually support our contention that the bill was ill-conceived in the first place, simplistic, and too far-reaching.

The Assembly of First Nations has consistently stated that Bill C-27 is misguided legislation that belies a broken relationship between the Government of Canada and First Nations – a relationship that continues to be characterized by federal direction, interference, and imposition on First Nations governments, our common message with respect to the federal government's overall approach to addressing the deficiencies of governance under the Indian Act through its own legislative agenda. Canada's approach, reflected in Bill C-27 – and also in Bills S-2 [Family Homes on Reserves and Matrimonial Interests or Rights Act], S-6 [First Nations Elections Act], and S-8 [An Act Respecting the Safety of Drinking Water on First Nations Lands] – is that the federal government has the right and, in fact, the responsibility to determine policy and draft legislation affecting our peoples on matters the government considers to be in our best interests and that it can do so with limited, or no, consultation. This approach persists, despite the existence and broad scope of our inherent right of self-government.

Canada argues that this bill, like the others, is good for us, good for our citizens, and good for the country – in the case of C-27, seeking to ensure increased transparency and accountability – and, therefore, the government says, who can argue with that?

Our perspective, as First Nations, reflected in our approach to Nation rebuilding, is quite different from Canada's – that is, our peoples have the right and, equally important, the responsibility to determine our own policy and make our own laws that govern our lands and peoples. As many witnesses to both the Commons and Senate Standing Committees have presented, C-27 is not the mechanism to improve or support accountability. It neither looks to developing standards or capacity to provide sound financial management nor reflects the work of our Nations to build financial administrative laws and appropriate supportive structures and processes.

Make no mistake, First Nations leaders are fully committed and supportive of transparency and accountability to their citizens. Our citizens demand it. Idle No More is not just about holding Canada to account for the plight of our peoples but also our own governments. In 2010, Chiefs-in-Assembly passed Resolution 50-2010: First Nation Governments Demonstrating Accountability, which states their commitment to maintaining transparent and accountable decision-making structures and also confirmed that their primary reporting and accountability relationship is to their citizens, not Canada. This resolution was not implying support for Bill C-27.

Financial transparency and accountability are aspects of a much broader accountability framework that is part of our Nation-rebuilding agenda. All federal legislation that concerns our peoples' interests, including C-27, must support this agenda and our transition from essentially being wards of the state under the Indian Act to self-governing peoples with responsibility for good governance, including designing, establishing, and then enforcing our own accountability mechanisms.

Those of us who live on reserve and understand the challenges of re-building are not naive – it is not a simple undertaking to undo 150 years of colonization and rebuild. The truth is, we all have a responsibility to work together to find solutions that facilitate this transition and not simply to say it is too hard or that we tried and then use that excuse to take the position that the government is currently taking – to design our post-Indian Act governance structures for us. As I have said before, this is neocolonialism and an inappropriate use of federal legislative power and will simply continue to challenge the relationship that exists between Canada and First Nations.

Reflecting on our January 11 meeting with Prime Minister Harper, in discussing the transition from the Indian Act, the Prime Minister responded to our criticisms of his government's actions and challenged our leadership by asking for solutions. One solution – one option – is Bill S-212: An Act Providing for the Recognition of Self-Governing First Nations of Canada, which, of course, was introduced by the former chair of this committee, Senator St. Germain, late last year and, in short, is a mechanism to facilitate a new relationship.

My colleague, Terry Goodtrack, president of the Aboriginal Financial Officers Association, provided similar evidence to you last week in terms of the relationship between the Government of Canada and First Nations. Specifically, he spoke about the fiscal relationship. So, too, did another respected colleague, Harold Calla, chair of the Financial Management Board (FMB), an institution that is a result of another First Nations–led solution. Under the First Nations Fiscal and Statistical Management Act (FSMA), the power of a First Nation to make a financial administration law, or FAL, is recognized. Under FMB's standards, a FAL addresses all of the substantive policy matters contained in Bill C-27, other than the regressive provisions dealing with the powers of the minister to publish internal documents of a First Nation or that seek to enforce administrative and legal remedies against any First Nation that does not comply with the terms of the bill.

In my own community, We Wai Kai, as I presented to the Commons Committee, when we learned about Bill C-27 (then Bill C-575), we decided to enact a FAL under the FSMA, which we have now done. As we transition away from the Indian Act and develop our own economy, our own-source revenues are increasing, so it is important that there be a robust financial framework for how we, as a community, budget, expend, and account for that expenditure. Our FAL is far more comprehensive than what is covered by Bill C-27.

Similarly, all self-government agreements set out that a First Nation will establish internal financial administration arrangements comparable to those of other governments within the Confederation. They also typically refer to the First Nation following generally accepted accounting principles, or GAAP. First Nations agree to operate like any other government within Canada, including the treatment of related business entities. But they design their own systems.

While C-27 also speaks to transparency and accountability to First Nation citizens, the bill reaches further and has different policy objectives. The requirement for public posting on a First Nations website – along with posting on the Aboriginal Affairs and Northern Development Canada website and the allowance for any person, not just a member of a First Nation, to apply to a court for disclosure of financial statements and salary reports, along with the increased enforcement powers of the minister – reflects additional and increased public scrutiny and greater federal oversight and control.

First Nations are already required to report on matters covered in this bill through their funding agreements with the federal government. The statutory requirement for public disclosure of salaries, including from related entities, in a schedule of remuneration is reaching. In truth, it is only one aspect to the relationship between our business entities and our governments, which is far more complicated and involved than just about disclosing salaries and wages that might be paid to Chief and council – namely, how investment decisions are made, what type of economic activity the Nation is undertaking, and the risk tolerance the Nation has if it is guaranteeing an enterprise.

In short, First Nations governments and their related entities should financially report and account in a manner comparable to other governments and their entities in Canada, but under our own law. In this spirit, therefore, in addition to the exemption for self-governing First Nations, there should also be an exemption in C-27 for a First Nation that has made a FAL under the FSMA.

Before I close, I want to make it clear: the Assembly of First Nations and First Nations governments had no involvement in the development of this bill. There are obligations on Canada for consultation, and it is unfortunate that we do not have a clear process or agreed-to mechanism to ensure First Nations involvement.

The AFN welcomes the calls from some honourable senators and previous witnesses for this bill to be withdrawn. In its current form, Bill C-27 will do little to practically support true First Nations accountability or Nation rebuilding but will simply further impose federal rules upon First Nations governments. In addition, there is the real potential for legal challenge if Canada continues to impose legislation on First Nations without meaningful consultation.

Accountability should be supported through recognizing and supporting the efforts of our governments as they rebuild their institutions and financial policies and practices. A focus of legislators should be on mechanisms for increasing the options available to First Nations to develop and implement our own governance structures, including accountability frameworks, so they can build their own future within Canada rather than be legislated from above.

Bill S-212, while not existing in its final form, is an option that needs to be studied thoroughly, and does, in my opinion, represent the promise of an appropriate use of the Crown's legislative powers, one that supports and empowers the exercise of self-determination by our Nations based on recognition and reconciliation and on the principle of free, prior, and informed consent of our citizens. The solutions that are working – and we are making progress on different fronts – are being found by working together, by creating the space and tools for communities to rebuild and move through that postcolonial door. It is the government's choice and opportunity to work with us on these solutions, rather than impose its own. Otherwise, for many of our Nations that door will never truly be opened.

Developing a New Fiscal Relationship

Adapted from an address to BC First Nations Fiscal Dialogue,
"A Continued Dialogue on 'Defining a New First Nations Fiscal
Relationship with the Crown,'" October 13, 2017

We are now in the centre, the centre of a transition that our country is going through to fully implement UNDRIP, to give meaning to section 35, and to implementing the inherent right of self-government – creating opportunity and supporting positive change in our communities. For me, as both a federal politician and as an Indigenous person, it is interesting to see how the media has been reporting about how our government is moving too slowly on the so-called Indigenous file. The prevailing narrative suggests we are doing very little. To anyone in our world who is truly engaged in Nation rebuilding and knows, historically, how much time and effort it has taken in the past to get things done, you know, of course, this is not true.

But I do get it. And to be a bit provocative, it is a narrative that, unfortunately, is all too often promulgated by Indigenous pundits or activists who seem to have little real understanding about the change required to make a difference back home in our communities, or where perpetuating the good fight is perhaps seen as more important or easier politically than recognizing real progress. For me, this is where the proverbial rubber of political rhetoric meets the road – in this case, the road to and from the reserve. For those of us who have been in the trenches and working at this a long time, it is not about shouting at the flat tire and thinking it will get fixed but rather having the tools to fix it yourself. It is about empowerment. It is about rebuilding – Nation rebuilding.

And in supporting the path to self-determination, changing the way the government does business – getting our house in order, as the Prime Minister said at the UN General Assembly a few weeks ago – takes time and was, is, a necessary step in making transformative change, to changing patterns of behaviour so we can move initiatives forward in a timely manner. For those of you who know how painstakingly long it took to get the Framework Agreement on First Nation Land Management negotiated and then implemented, or to set up the First Nations Finance Authority (FNFA), or to get the First Nations Tax Commission (FNTC) out of the department, you know exactly what I am talking about. The pace of change now, to some of you, must seem remarkable – despite the naysayers. And this is why we need more leaders like you, people who understand what needs to be done and why it has been so hard in the past, who understand that while it will not always be easy going forward, it will be easier than when you built your institutions, which are still, of course, works in progress and with their own legacy issues.

So, we all need to continue to be strong proponents for change, to continue to be courageous and take bold steps, to not be apologetic or defensive.

As part of our government's role in supporting change and the necessary reforms, the Prime Minister formed a working group of federal ministers to review laws, policies, and operational practices. I was very honoured to be asked to chair the working group, and I have been working very hard with my colleagues to pursue an ambitious agenda for reform. The working group is very real, and I can tell you the ministers who sit on the working group are motivated, keen, and can sense they are a part of something transformative, something important, something big. One of the first steps the working group took was to release ten "Principles Respecting the Government of Canada's Relationship with Indigenous Peoples." The goal of the principles is pretty straightforward – to trigger a definitive departure from the denial of rights, disempowerment, and assimilation to a place of recognition.

Something that was instilled in me from a very young age and that has been confirmed in my work over the years is this: colonialism cannot be stemmed and ultimately overcome without the recognition and implementation of the inherent rights of Indigenous Peoples. Accordingly, the principles are the necessary starting point for a recognition-based approach to changing federal laws, policies, and operational practices through engagement with you. They are rooted in section 35 and the UN Declaration and are informed by the Truth and Reconciliation Commission's calls to action as well as the report of the Royal Commission on Aboriginal Peoples. At the core of the ten principles is the recognition of Indigenous Peoples, governments, and laws and their relationship to lands and resources. The principles affirm the right to self-determination, the inherent right of self-government, and Indigenous governments as distinct orders of government. They are explicit in rejecting certain long-standing federal positions – such as a focus on extinguishment, surrender, or denial of rights – and are clear that all relationships must be based on the recognition and implementation of rights.

They also speak to the need for a new fiscal relationship that actually supports Indigenous governments to exercise their right to self-determination. While all of the principles speak to and in some way support the building of Indigenous institutions, two of the principles speak directly to this work and the need for new fiscal arrangements that will enable Indigenous governments to develop beyond the confines imposed by the Indian Act and build on the work of the First Nations Fiscal Management Act. Principle 4 recognizes that Indigenous self-government is part of Canada's evolving system of cooperative federalism and distinct orders of government. It lays the groundwork for ensuring, based on recognition of rights, the space for the operation of Indigenous jurisdictions, institutions, and laws and the creation of new mechanisms and institutions to bring these postcolonial structures and processes to life. Principle 8 recognizes that reconciliation and self-government require a renewed fiscal relationship, developed in collaboration with Indigenous Nations, that promotes a mutually supportive climate for economic partnership and resource development. It recognizes that the rights, interests, perspectives, and governance role of Indigenous

Peoples are central to securing a new fiscal relationship. It also recognizes the importance of strong Indigenous governments in achieving political, social, economic, and cultural development and improved quality of life.

The ten principles are, like the working group, real – they are serious, not nuanced. And while some may be skeptical – for instance, trying to see some hidden intent where the principles might deviate somewhat from the text from UNDRIP – I can assure you from my vantage point that there is no hidden intent. In accordance with Article 38 of UNDRIP, which sets out that "states, in consultation and cooperation with Indigenous peoples, shall take the appropriate measures, including legislative measures, to achieve the ends of this Declaration," our government will continue to support and strengthen those mechanisms that already exist and are working, along with supporting the development of new mechanisms to ensure a more efficient and rapid transformation of Indigenous Nations, including getting rid of the Indian Act as quickly as possible.

This is why, after establishing the working group and then adopting the principles, our Prime Minister took the next and significant step of dividing the former department of Indigenous and Northern Affairs Canada (INAC) into two separate and distinct departments. This is a necessary step in dismantling many of the problematic governance structures that have held our Nations back for far too long and that have hindered the growth of strong, independent Indigenous institutions and self-governance structures, which are now beginning to take hold. These are just the early steps towards a vision of Indigenous self-governance that will transcend the barriers enshrined in the Indian Act and enable leaders like yourselves to develop new and stronger Indigenous institutions that will support our communities to flourish and prosper. And while there are grey areas to sort out in the dismantling of INAC, I think it is safe to say that the sectoral governance initiatives will be on the self-determination side – that is, with the Minister of Crown–Indigenous Relations and Northern Affairs. Although I do see a role for Indigenous institutions taking over work within the Indigenous Services department during this period of transition.

On this note, I am aware of the Lands Advisory Board's proposal that there needs to be a more general recognition of self-government that is concomitant with the recognition of land management powers, and then not just applicable on reserve. While we all need to be mindful of how we address the question of the proper title and rights holder and how we build self-government out from imposed governance structures, there is much merit to this proposal. In my opinion, you cannot really be self-governing if you do not manage and govern over lands, and you cannot really manage lands unless you are self-governing. I agree that we need to ensure that we set the tone for what we mean by self-government and inherent rights and not let the courts do this for us.

Likewise with respect to fiscal matters. Clearly the ten principles call for a new fiscal relationship. The Department of Finance was a part of developing the principles. There is no question that Indigenous governments need the "ways and means for financing their autonomous functions," as set out in Article 4 of UNDRIP. So, to the fiscal institutions – your suggestions are important and timely. Your "Principles to Guide a New First Nations–Crown Fiscal Relationship" are very helpful to show the tremendous work being done here in BC.

And keeping on the subject of new fiscal relations, I am also aware there are two parallel tables ongoing right now. One is with the Assembly of First Nations. The second table is with Indigenous self-governments, those nations that are self-governing, along with a connected table for those negotiating agreements. This second group is working with federal officials to develop a new federal fiscal policy with respect to Indigenous self-governments. In my view, at some point all this work will need to be coordinated and the fiscal relationship considered within the sectoral governance context, not just from the federal end but also from the Indigenous end.

Ultimately, all paths lead down the same road of self-determination. Again, I am not sure where it all ends or how it plays out – the final destination – but what I do know is that without taking the steps together, we will never get there. I also know it is a road along which there can be no turning back. This is our collective responsibility – both an opportunity and a challenge. There are people back home who are counting on us. Canadians generally are counting on us because they, too, want a better life for Indigenous Peoples and cannot believe in this day and age we still have boil-water advisories in dozens of communities.

And, of course, there are the skeptics and the naysayers we must prove wrong. As you already have done in creating the institutions you all represent here today, let us prove them wrong even more by making them and others even stronger and even more successful.

So, my friends, no pressure!

Let me leave you with these thoughts. Change comes through action and not just words, and it is never easy. Nothing worthwhile doing ever is. We – Canada and Indigenous Nations – all have a lot of work to do, and it will be very challenging.

There is a standing invitation to all Indigenous Peoples across the country to share perspectives and ideas on priority federal laws, policies, and operational practices that the review should address. I have no illusions as this process unfolds about how difficult it will be for the federal system to adjust. Likewise, I know how hard it will be for many Indigenous Nations. Hard choices and creativity will be needed across government and within Indigenous communities to transform this work into meaningful and lasting change, into practical benefits on the ground. As leaders with a proven capacity for building institutions and structures to support self-governance, you are at the forefront of these changes, demonstrating how transformative they can truly be. I am counting on leaders like yourselves to continue to be key partners and allies in this important and exciting period of transformation.

The stage is set.

The Governance Toolkit
and Building on OUR Success

Adapted from *BCAFN Governance Toolkit: A Guide to Nation Building*, 2nd ed., "Letter from Regional Chief Jody Wilson-Raybould" and Foreword to Part 1, *The Governance Report* (West Vancouver: British Columbia Assembly of First Nations, 2014).

The British Columbia Assembly of First Nations' *Governance Toolkit: A Guide to Nation Building* is a comprehensive guide intended to assist Nations in building or rebuilding governance and navigating their way out from under the Indian Act at their own pace and based on their own priorities. Since it was first conceived, this project has taken on a life of its own and continues to grow. The *Governance Toolkit* also continues the work of previous BC Regional Chiefs and draws on the growing governance experiences of Nations in BC, working together to improve the lives of our people.

The project of Nation building or rebuilding, and ongoing reconciliation with the federal and provincial governments as part of that project, is not simply some political or legal exercise backed up by an academic argument about rights and reclaiming power. Rather, it reflects a deep understanding among First Nations leaders and citizens that strong and appropriate governance is truly necessary if First Nations are to reach their full potential with their citizens' opportunities maximized and their collective future as Indigenous Peoples within Confederation certain.

Simply defined, "governance" means "establishing rules to coordinate our actions and achieve our goals." As societies, the institutions we create to make rules and then enforce them, we call "government." Governance and government come in many forms but are always needed. They can, of course, be done well or badly. Research and experts tell us that the quality of governance, much more than its specific form, has a huge impact on the fortunes of any given society. Ours are no exception. Societies that govern well simply do better economically, socially, and politically than those that do not. Strong and appropriate governance increases a society's chances of effectively meeting the needs of its people.

In many diverse ways, based on our different cultures and traditions, this is exactly what our peoples did for centuries before the arrival of Europeans. The reality that we lived in productive, sustainable, and viable societies is a testament to the fact that our governing systems worked. With the arrival of the newcomers, all this quickly changed. While we may have had some form of government under the Indian Act, we were for the most part denied the powers (jurisdictions) we needed to govern and the governing institutions that could exercise power effectively.

During the colonial period, our governments were based on models developed by the federal government to deliver its programs and services. The powers of our governments were very limited. The effects on us were unfortunate, as the Indian Act system promoted an impoverished concept of government. "Government" for us became little more than managing programs (education, health, housing, social assistance, etc.) and distributing limited resources (money, jobs, influence, and services). The concept of government as being about making laws, resolving disputes, and generating the means to pursue a collective vision was smothered by the need for federal programs and services and the fact that the local "band office" was the instrument to deliver them.

Thankfully, this is changing, and a more robust concept of governance based on Indigenous legal traditions is re-emerging as we slowly rebuild strong and appropriate governance. This is happening for many reasons. One reason is the advancement of our right to self-determination, both domestically through section 35 of the Constitution Act, 1982, and internationally through the United Nations Declaration on the Rights of Indigenous Peoples. It is also a reflection of the growing political realization – not just among us but among others – that our Nations truly need strong and appropriate governance in order to succeed. Finally, this is happening because our Nations are increasingly raising more of their own revenues to provide strong governance.

In BC, our Nations are leading the way. Among them, they have made over 2,500 contemporary bylaws and laws, and they are the leaders in numerous sectoral and comprehensive governance initiatives in Canada along a continuum of governance reform. Governance is being exercised on "Lands reserved for Indians," treaty settlement lands, and Aboriginal Title Lands, as well as on ancestral lands that transcend all other categories of First Nation lands.

The *Governance Toolkit* draws on all of this work in postcolonial governance and brings it together in one document. The core of the toolkit is Part 1, *The Governance Report,* which takes a comprehensive look at options for governance reform and considers, subject by subject, the powers (jurisdictions) of Nations. The report is written from the perspective that the Nation is the building block of governance and that our Nations have the inherent right to govern. It looks at how we are moving in this direction along a continuum of governance options and reforms by providing a snapshot of what our Nations in BC are actually doing on the ground to support and create strong and appropriate governance. It is of particular use to First Nations communities and community leaders in developing their Nations' own "critical paths" to implementing governance reform and re-establishing or establishing governance for their peoples and lands and, if necessary, engaging in reconciliation discussions with the Crown.

The report poses important questions on governance and presents options: What are the rules needed to coordinate a Nation's priorities and achieve its goals? What are the institutions a First Nation requires to make these rules and then enforce them? The appropriate answers to these questions will, of course, depend on each First Nation's priorities and particular circumstances.

The report covers a range of options currently available to First Nations in undertaking or approaching governance reform. The options, along what we call the "governance continuum," include governance reform under the Indian Act, reform as part of sectoral governance initiatives, and recognized governance reform through comprehensive governance arrangements made with the federal government and, where appropriate, the

Government of British Columbia. The report also addresses other options for implementing First Nations governance beyond the Indian Act that are being contemplated or are under development.

Part 2, *The Governance Self-Assessment,* comprises two modules that Nations can use to evaluate the effectiveness of their institutions of governance and the effectiveness of their administration. Part 3, *A Guide to Community Engagement: Navigating Our Way through the Post-colonial Door,* assists Nations in beginning or continuing discussions with their citizens about the importance of strong and appropriate governance and options for governance reform, including moving beyond the Indian Act.

I am pleased to say that the *Governance Toolkit* has been developed in-house by the BCAFN with the support and contributions of many individuals and organizations. Drafts were reviewed by peer groups, and the self-assessment modules were piloted in a number of communities and revised extensively following insightful dialogue. Moving forward, it is essential that First Nations have governance choices, share information, and build on the experience and work of other First Nations. By assembling First Nations governance stories all in one place, in a way that is both accessible and logically organized, the report is helping First Nations sort through the governance options.

The *Governance Toolkit* was written from the perspective that the primary relationship between First Nations and the Crown is through the federal government in light of section 91(24) of the Constitution Act, 1867, which assigns the federal government primary responsibility for "Indians, and Lands reserved for the Indians." Subject to any governance arrangements negotiated with the Crown, or a court ordering that the Indian Act or parts of it are unconstitutional for infringing on the inherent right of self-government, Canada governs "Lands reserved for the Indians" and "Indians" through the Indian Act and other statutes and in doing so creates a "fiduciary" relationship with First Nations. This will only change if Canada, after considering our interests, has the political will to enact legislation to amend or repeal the Indian Act and alter its application to reserves and "Indians." It is important not to let the federal fiduciary responsibility become a barrier to progress, and it is important that First Nations reconcile the fiduciary relationship with their Nation-building or rebuilding processes.

In addition, recent developments in the law suggest that the strict constitutional division of powers between the federal and provincial governments may not be so hard and fast or important and that, indeed, provincial governments may have equal, if not more, responsibility with respect to First Nations peoples, and certainly with respect to governance matters beyond reserve lands and within the broader ancestral lands of a Nation. The evolving relationship between First Nations and the Crown (both federal and provincial) must be kept in mind as questions of multilevel governance are being answered and reconciled and as First Nations rebuild.

In many cases, reconciliation negotiations with the Crown, with either the federal government or the provincial government, or both, will be necessary for moving forward. Simply navigating the bureaucracy and the evolving governance-related processes can be a significant part of the challenge. The *Governance Report* therefore considers the requirements of the various processes that have been established to facilitate moving out from under the Indian Act with respect to on-reserve governance or that consider governance with respect to ancestral lands. In some cases, processes have been led, designed, and mainly controlled by First Nations. In others, and depending on the scope and geographical application of the proposed governance arrangements, the process has been managed by either Canada, through Aboriginal Affairs and Northern Development Canada, or the province. In some cases, all parties to the negotiations jointly develop the processes with other bodies that have been established to assist.

We have come a long way. This journey is reflected in the fact that this report could not exist if the options for governance reform did not exist. However, we still have a lot of work to do to create the legal and political space within Canada to fully implement the inherent right of self-government and realize our collective vision, which is ultimately to make the lives of our people better. What we have learned is that transforming Indian Act governance is no small task. After more than a century of living under the Indian Act, it may be difficult for some Nations, as indeed it has been for the federal government, to shed the routine of colonialism and tackle the seemingly overwhelming task of Nation building or Nation rebuilding. For some, the status quo works and, unfortunately, serves their self-interest. For others, it may be hard to shed the old ways. Many more will simply be afraid of change, preferring to live "with the devil they know rather than with the one they do not." At times, there will be tensions between current and traditional practices, and it will be a challenge to reconcile them. What is encouraging, though, is that despite the challenges, many of Nations have already walked through, or are walking through, the postcolonial door, are reconciling with the Crown, and are establishing strong and appropriate governance with their own institutions of governance and the range of powers they need to govern. While considerable work remains, we are well on our way to realizing our collective vision.

Building Business
Relationships and the
Duty to Consult

"

How free, prior, and informed consent
is sought and given is, at the core, the central challenge
operating at many levels for government, industry,
and our Nations.

"

Economic Development
Depends on Self-Government

Adapted from paper presented at Canadian Council for Aboriginal Business, Aboriginal Business Forum, "Building Sustainable Business," March 31, 2010

What is the role of First Nations governments in building business? All levels or orders of government in Canada have important roles to play in helping rebuild First Nations economies, but it is our governments, First Nations governments, who arguably have the greatest role – and not just with respect to our reserve-based economies, but beyond. And we need the tools to do it.

Strengthening the First Nations economy will strengthen the Canadian economy and provide opportunities for not only First Nations businesses but also non-Aboriginal businesses. Canada is currently coming out of one of the worst recessions in modern world history, and we are doing somewhat better than our neighbours to the south and the other Western liberal democracies. When the current recession began and governments around the globe began talking about "economic stimulus," many of our Aboriginal leaders said First Nations have always been in a state of recession and in need of stimulus. This was a statement about the health of the majority of First Nations economies and the lack of participation by our own people in our own economies and within the broader Canadian economy generally.

While important, it is not just about stimulus and the need for money. Economic health is determined by the type of polices and the laws made by governments and the politics of those governments. But you all know this. Your businesses and companies no doubt support government that understands what is needed for your companies to compete in a global marketplace. You support and donate to the political parties of your choice, and you can influence public policy in many ways. Within this world of politics and economics, non-Aboriginal government is already well established with a legal framework that has been developed over hundreds of years, reflecting the will of the people and the policy and priorities of those who influence and control the government. Today, we take for granted our modern market economy and the legal and political framework that supports it.

First Nations governments are not like other governments in Canada. Our system of government is in a state of transition. For years, we have been under federal administrative authority, and our people and our economies have been governed separate and apart from non-Aboriginal Canada through the Indian Act. Thankfully, however, this is all changing, but not fast enough. And why is this changing? Because there are people like yourselves, and Aboriginal leaders and federal and provincial politicians, who have supported legislative initiatives to replace the Indian Act. They have supported the negotiation of governance as part of modern land claims or in the context of pre-existing treaties to facilitate the transition from Indian Act government to appropriate government for today's world, government, where a First Nation so chooses, that is supportive of private-sector investment.

In order for First Nations people to make the most of opportunities on existing reserve lands and contribute to the broader economy, the system of government and the legal framework needs to be changed from the ground up. But this is also true for off-reserve Indigenous Peoples and within the Traditional Territories of our First Nations – within a treaty territory or a territory of unextinguished Aboriginal Title.

The courts have established a principle that the Crown must consult and accommodate First Nations where Aboriginal Rights are impacted. This is changing the way government, and by implication, industry deals with First Nations. In my province, BC, it is almost next to impossible for a significant development to take place within the Traditional Territory of a First Nation without the meaningful involvement of the First Nations. So, it raises the questions: With whom do you consult and perhaps enter into an accommodation or benefits agreement? And when business or industry so desire, with whom do you enter into a business relationship?

And so I return to my main point – in the absence of appropriate governance at the First Nations or tribal level, it is not only difficult to know with whom you are expected to do business but also whether the political and legal structure of the group you are dealing with has the authority or political legitimacy to engage with you. This is a serious problem for First Nations if we are to take advantage of opportunities and develop our economies but also, now, a serious problem for the Crown and industry. To put it another way, the very limitations of Indian Act government, which hindered the ability of our Nations to develop economies on our reserve lands, are now the same impediments to engaging with industry and businesses off reserve within our broader Traditional Territories, therefore impacting the broader economy.

So what are we doing about this?

In my province, I was elected to the BC Assembly of First Nations on a platform that focuses on four interrelated areas: (1) the establishment of strong and appropriate governance, (2) fair land and resources settlements (a huge issue in BC, where we do not have settlements), (3) improved education, and (4) individual health. The last two are a recognition that we cannot take advantage of opportunities if we do not have a healthy and well-educated citizenry. My focus here is, of course, on governance. There are a number of legislative opportunities – the First Nations Land Management Act, the First Nations Oil and Gas and Moneys Management Act, and other initiatives – that support the necessary transition from Indian Act governments, either sectorally or comprehensively. But for real change to occur in a meaningful and broad way, all our communities must go through their own process of local transformation, healing, rebuilding, call it what you may. Our colonial period must officially end.

This is a process that cannot be dictated by the federal government or any other external organization. Change will not be initiated through federal civil servants or bureaucrats, however well meaning. At its core, this is a political process of change that starts with us: First Nations. Change will come from the people who are directly and significantly affected. This means the citizens of our communities, the business leaders who have a mutual interest in seeing stable and appropriate government, and other Canadians. It will, of course, require continued federal government and, where appropriate, provincial government support. There will be need for future legislation. This is a mammoth task and not one to be undertaken lightly. There are 633 First Nations or bands in Canada, and 203 in my province.

At the BCAFN, we are developing what we are calling "A Governance Engagement and Assessment Tool" for First Nations, which will help communities begin this process of transformation if they have not already started or, if they have, to refine their plan, so that our leaders and our citizens, with the support of their staff, can begin the process of deconstructing their current Indian Act reality and begin laying a path for post-Indian Act governance, for building the institutions they need to govern and make decisions. It is the vision that every community will be able to have this conversation and begin moving forward with their own colonial "exit" strategy.

This will take leadership. It will also take financial resources. Business and industry have the opportunity to invest in the rebuilding of our governments, where doing so will undoubtedly create a better business climate on reserve and provide certainty off reserve.

I would ask the members of the Canadian Council for Aboriginal Business to seriously look at ways that your companies and your organization can support the establishment of strong and appropriate governance in our communities. Of course, I know many of you already do and are helping in different ways. This is also a call to our Aboriginal business leaders. You, too, have a continued role to play in ensuring our governments are properly constituted and run well. We all have a role to play and an interest in supporting First Nations during this transition period. In the BC region, as we roll out our community-based governance engagement and assessment tool, we will be looking for support and help, so someday, when we meet as an Assembly of First Nations, it truly is an assembly of postcolonial First Nations.

In moving forward with governance reform, we should never lose sight of the underlying objective. Economic development and business success are not the end in themselves but rather a means to an end, the end being healthier and more prosperous First Nations communities.

First Nations Are Not a Box to Tick Off

Adapted from a presentation to the Canadian Aboriginal Minerals
Association annual conference, "Meeting Minds, Making Mines: Aboriginal
Community Development through the Mining Sector," November 7, 2011

As Aboriginal Title and Rights continue to be recognized on the ground, it is fair to say that there cannot be any major mining or development activity within our territories without First Nations involvement. There is the need for the free, prior, and informed consent of the Aboriginal Title holder before Indigenous property rights are impacted. This is required under international law and has been advanced in our domestic courts. How free, prior, and informed consent is sought and given is, at the core, the central challenge operating at many levels for government, industry, and our Nations.

To put this evolving reality into perspective, we have never had a period in this province's and Canada's history where there has been so much planned mining development and other major capital investment since Aboriginal Rights have been established and the duties on the Crown confirmed. When all of the major mining and development projects in BC were undertaken primarily in the 1950s, '60s, and '70s, there was no section 35 in the Constitution Act recognizing Aboriginal and Treaty Rights, there were limited court decisions respecting what Aboriginal Title and Rights meant, concepts such as consultation and accommodation were not in the lexicon and, for the most part, major development projects proceeded without our involvement and certainly not with our free, prior, and informed consent. Our peoples were essentially the forgotten people at the end of gravel roads. This is no longer the case.

Today, there is a resurgence of planned mining and resource extraction and billions of dollars of planned investment. BC Premier Christy Clark announced only a few weeks ago that eight new mines are planned in the coming years, not to mention huge and, for the most part, controversial resource projects such as the Site C Dam on the Peace River, the Enbridge Northern Gateway project, significant transmission line expansion, Prosperity Mine, the Kinder Morgan expansion, and two liquid natural gas depots that are all front and centre in the news. Despite the current blip in the world economy, the global appetite for natural resources is increasing as foreign investors look to our soils to either purchase our resource companies, partner, or sign long-term contracts for delivery of product. We simply have not had this level and kind of proposed activity in a post-legal world of *Delgamuukw* (1997), *Haida* (2004), and *Taku* (2004). I know this is probably not news and, of course, your companies and our Nations are trying to work through what this means practically on the ground to support sustainable mining exploration and development moving forward. First Nations are not, on principle, opposed to mining or development, but not at any cost.

While in the past denial and delay may have been the preferred political strategy of government, as opposed to having to make publicly unpopular choices to support the resolution of "land claims," today there is really no choice. While, facetiously, one could say that "the chickens have now come home to roost," in truth, reconciliation will be good for all British Columbians, as will the sustainable economic development that follows.

As Aboriginal Title and Rights crystallize on the ground with new court decisions and demands for justice at the regional, national, and international levels, it is also not surprising that Premier Clark is rightfully worried that the BC treaty-making process is taking too long and that her government is focusing instead on "striking economic development deals with Native leaders who are willing to do business," as reported in the *Globe* last week. It is no secret that the BC government is politically banking on the ambitious and unprecedented level of investment in major development projects over the coming years and the new jobs hopefully created. It is not surprising for anyone intimately involved in treaty negotiations that deals have had to be made outside of the treaty process. BC officials must now act where there is a reasonable presumption of Aboriginal Title, and thus agreements need to be reached. There is incentive and motivation. For legal reasons, BC cannot wait for a treaty. In fact, economically, neither can First Nations, nor do most want to. Also, in truth, unless there are significant changes to the BC treaty-making process and in particular the approaches taken by Canada and BC to substantive issues at the table – their mandates – it is unlikely, in my opinion, that there will be many more treaties, if any, other than those that are very close to completion. This is unfortunate but true.

But be under no illusion, notwithstanding the present issues with the BC treaty-making process and the new focus of the Premier, settlement of the land question remains fundamental for all our Nations in BC and all citizens. While it is certainly positive that Premier Clark wants to deal and is prepared to deal and is dealing outside of treaty making, a word of caution is in order.

Simply doing business with the willing cannot be a substitute for resolution of the land question with the many. The current inability to reach fair and meaningful settlements with the majority of our Nations through treaties or otherwise cannot be held out as a reason to step back from the broader objectives of reconciliation and the need to find ways to settle the "land question" once and for all. We cannot give up because it is too hard. We need to understand the impediments to settlement. This requires a high-level commitment, not only from Premier Clark but also from Canada as well, as a significant amount of fundamental community development work is needed on the ground in our villages to complete the slow and often painful process of decolonization.

From my perspective, we need to refocus our efforts on community-led governance reform. In the absence of appropriate governance at the First Nations or tribal level it is not only difficult to know who may give free, prior, and informed consent but also whether the political and legal structure of the group you are dealing with has the authority and political legitimacy to engage with you. Are they the proper Aboriginal Title holder? This is a serious problem for First Nations if we are to take advantage of opportunities and develop our economies, but it is also, now, a serious problem for the Crown and industry. The impoverished system of governance under the Indian Act is not only weak and inappropriate but simply not capable of supporting the types of decision making and responsibility that recognition of Aboriginal Title demands. It is only with strong and appropriate government that our Nations can truly engage with the Crown and third parties in a postcolonial world and legitimately represent the views of the Nation in making difficult and potentially controversial decisions respecting our position or involvement in major economic development projects, including mining projects.

For its part, Canada must revisit its policy with respect to self-government and "land claims" so that it is consistent with domestic and international law, and Canada must support our Nations' rebuilding our governing institutions post-Indian Act forthwith and certainly not wait for and make governance reform conditional on signing a treaty. Did you know that if a community is ready to move beyond Indian Act governance, it may actually be held hostage under the Indian Act until a treaty is reached? Did you also know that Canada unilaterally assesses the readiness of our communities to move beyond the Indian Act and, consequently, has become a bureaucratic gatekeeper to social and political reform and justice being served?

The BC government, for its part, has to continue to increase revenue sharing with all our Nations and to ensure fair access to lands and resources that supports Nation building and good governance. The province needs to ensure during this period of transition that it does not discriminate and deals with all Nations within the existing, if imperfect, institutions and structures. In fact, there is a moral, if not legal, imperative to go above and beyond with our Nations in transition, to ensure that the province's obligations with respect to consultation and accommodation are met. The province must also pressure Canada to stop dragging its feet on land claims settlement and ensure that Canada supports governance reform. It is the people of this province that suffer the most when Canada's policies do not allow it to act quickly or respond to our issues and the opportunities. The BC government has more at stake than Canada, so it should really be pressuring Canada politically to step up to the plate and do the right thing.

For our part, our Nations need to continue our governance reform as well as resolve issues of shared territory and overlap, which have always, historically, existed but during the colonial period have been complicated by the creation of reserves and Indian Act governance. Without knowing who speaks with authority for the proper Aboriginal Title holder there can be no certainty. Most importantly, we need to ensure our people are behind the change and supporting our legitimate and recognized governments. There is, as all of us who live and work back home know, a great fear of change, despite the terrible impacts of the Indian Act system – "the devil you know rather than the one you do not," a sentiment reflective of the fact that many of our people fear we will make the same mistakes as the colonizer did and establish systems of governance that are not fair or accountable and without proper controls. However, we also do not want anarchy. Without the support of our citizens, there can be no true progress – as, ultimately, it is the people in each of our villages that have to vote the colonial system of government out and say what replaces it.

So, we all need to work together – the federal government, the province, and First Nations – with common purpose to reinvent the land claims process. While the task of reconciliation is complicated, now is the time to act, and all parties must be up to the task. The seriousness of what is at stake for all British Columbians is no longer in question. It is not without significance that BC has been declared one of the worst jurisdictions to undertake mining exploration and development because of the failure to adequately address Aboriginal Rights in a country that legally protects them. So, commensurate with the seriousness of the problem, appropriate resources (in terms of people and time based on true commitment and priority) are needed. We need the best this country and province have to offer in terms of problem solvers and negotiators to work to find the solutions and to take charge. We need adequate resources – not simply money to support an industry of low-level negotiation with little chance of results that go on and on and on and, ironically, delay resolution.

Moving forward, it is also important that no community or Nation is left out or behind, because the social and political consequences of doing so would be intolerable. If conditions in some Nations improve while in others they do not, this will lead to a new level of social unrest. We have a responsibility to all our Nations and not just those where the government of BC or industry might want to build a mine, establish a port, or construct a pipeline. Decolonization cannot just be a factor of "location, location, location."

For First Nation leaders, you all know that taking on the challenge and the work of governance reform at the band level is no easy task and can be politically risky. What is so encouraging, though, is that despite the challenges, over 70 percent of our Nations here in BC are involved in some form of governance-reform activity. We know that where reforms have been instituted, they are working. I would respectfully suggest that as we go down this route in BC, it is in the interests of industry to strongly lobby and petition the Government of Canada and, where necessary, the Province of BC to support this work. It is in your interest as well as ours that our Nations have strong and appropriate governance. Your economic fate is our economic fate, and our collective fate will be determined by whether our First Nations governance is effective. We need your help because there is no guarantee that Parliament will do the right thing vis-à-vis the Indian Act and our proposals for change without yours and other Canadians' encouragement and political pressure.

And as with the caution to Premier Clark not to use the slow process of treaty negotiations as an excuse not to look for improved ways to comprehensively address the land question, so, too, we caution industry: just because our Nations are in a period of transition in terms of our governance, do not use this as a convenient excuse not to deal with our Nations or work with our communities in the present. In fact, it makes the activity and how you interact with our Nations even more significant given that it will not be until the larger challenges of rebuilding governance and settling claims are resolved that truly a new and enduring relationship will be established.

Simply just doing what the provincial and federal governments might tell you to do is not enough. The corporate choices you make today will determine your own fate, something that Taseko Mines is learning very clearly. I would like to leave industry reps with some parting thoughts on dealing with our Nations. There are a number of things companies can do now and certainly moving forward to build relationships and partnerships with our Nations.

1. While the crystallization of our title and rights now requires consultation with us and, in many cases, accommodation for our interests, please do not simply look at existing First Nations governments as an obstacle to resource extraction or a "box" to tick off on a checklist for what needs to be accomplished in order to get access to natural resources. I guarantee you that if you approach our issues in this way it is far less likely your project will ever succeed.

2. Assuming a First Nation government accepts a proposed project in principle, it is likely you will be asked to enter into a partnership of some sort and that this partnership can bring value to the overall project and therefore investors. This might be an equity stake.

3. Deal with First Nations early or first, before any other body or group.

4. Be prepared to scale back your expectations and timelines if there are concerns by our people, as represented by their governments, about the size and scope of the development activity. Our Nations will not accept development at any cost, even if they are going to benefit from revenue sharing or will be involved in some capacity with the actual business.

5. Please do not consider only the provincial or federal government as the authorizing body for resource development. As First Nations governance re-emerges and as we establish land-use plans and development guidelines within our Traditional Territories, our Nations' governments will increasingly become involved in the approval processes for natural resource extraction in our respective territories. There will be, and already is, in some cases, true shared decision-making examples in BC. This is a good thing. It provides certainty for all.

6. Please do not confuse the role of our leaders in their capacity as representatives of our governments and stewards of the lands with the role of our leaders (sometimes the same people, and sometimes not) who are involved in the business arms of our Nations – the development companies run by our First Nations or, indeed, run by our citizens as private enterprises. This is important, as these confusions can be easily made, where our governments are seen as both the approving body for resource development activities (the body with whom consultation is addressed) but also may be seen as the directors of the business arm of the First Nation, leading to potential conflicts of interest.

7. Notwithstanding issues you might have with a First Nation or group at any point in time, please support our ongoing efforts for governance reform and Nation building. Stronger Nations, properly constituted with clear powers and authority and the capacity to govern, will help ensure more meaningful engagement, leading to increased potential for lasting partnerships as well as meeting the evolving legal requirements for free, prior, and informed consent.

8. These considerations apply equally to First Nation–run businesses as they do to non-First Nation–run companies, whether the business activity takes place through community-owned enterprises or privately owned enterprises.

Each of us has a role to play and an interest in supporting First Nations during this transition period of Nation building or rebuilding. Yes, the colonial period has left scars. Yes, there is pain and anger. Yes, it can be politically unpopular to champion Indigenous Rights. This is no excuse, however, for inaction. Indigenous Rights are human rights, and while those of us alive today did not create the problems, we have it within our grasp to help solve them. When we inherit problems and then work around them, we risk becoming a part of the problem if we simply pass them on to someone else to solve. We have to be bigger than the problems. In Canada, there really can be no excuse for not resolving issues of appropriate and strong First Nations governance. We know what needs to be done, so let's do it. If not, as it has been in the past, there will be in the future questions about the legitimacy of decisions made today and continued uncertainty on the land.

Who Owns and Is Responsible for the Water?

Keynote address, "Watersheds 2014: Towards Watersheds
Governance in British Columbia and Beyond," January 23, 2014

Water is the lifeblood of this planet. Along with the air, it is the most important resource we all share. However, from the actions of governments around the world, one would be forgiven for thinking otherwise. There may be a UN Environmental Programme and UN resolutions on the human right to water and sanitation – indeed, there is a UN water rights special rapporteur – but it remains a global challenge for nation-states and their subnational governments to govern in a manner to ensure sustainable development and the protection of our natural resources – our inheritance.

We can do better. And Canada, with approximately 20 percent of the world's fresh water but where less than half is considered renewable, will have an important role to play in the international discussion around water use, governance, and management, a discussion that will only become more intense as global warming continues and as we continue to deplete our existing sources of nonrenewable fresh water. To meaningfully participate in this conversation internationally, with both authority and influence, Canada needs a more vigorous and informed discussion to develop a national vision and water strategy, one where our respective laws support and reflect that common vision.

In Canada, both the federal and provincial governments have constitutional responsibility for aspects of jurisdiction over water. Into this governance mix we must now, of course, consider the place of Aboriginal governments. As Aboriginal Peoples, we are in an exciting period of re-building – taking our rightful place within Confederation. To help understand Aboriginal issues with respect to water conceptually, I find it useful to make a distinction between (1) who "owns" the water and has access to it and (2) which laws govern the purveying of water from source to tap, notwithstanding who may legally own it.

Looking at questions of ownership first, under Western legal traditions, water is typically viewed as a commodity and can be owned. At common law, there are riparian rights. Indeed, water rights can be included in and run with grants to land. In BC, this was the case up until 1909, when water rights were, for the most part, removed from title and governed under separate statute, a statute the province still uses today (although woefully out of date) and is only now actively looking to update with the proposed Water Sustainability Act, expected to be introduced late February. In BC, there is, of course, still the outstanding "Indian land question" and issues of Aboriginal Rights, including Aboriginal Title or ownership of water. Simply stated, because there were few or no treaties through which our ancestral lands were lawfully acquired by the Crown, much of the lands and resources in BC remain subject to Aboriginal Title. While the courts have said, legally, Aboriginal Title exists, the question now is, Where and to what extent?

We may have an answer soon. This past November, the Supreme Court of Canada heard *Tsilhqot'in* (2014), a case concerning the Tŝilhqot'in title. We are awaiting the decision. Many believe the court will find that Aboriginal Title will not be the "small spots" or "postage stamp" areas that the province or Canada argued it should be, nor will it be the entire extent of the Traditional Territory that the Tŝilhqot'in occupied – rather it will be somewhere in between. But it will be significant and a lot larger area than the small reserves that were unilaterally set aside for us in the absence of treaty. My true hope is that *Tsilhqot'in* will create the impetus for true reconciliation, which has been so elusive despite the modern treaty-making process. *Tsilhqot'in*, however, is unlikely to answer conclusively the question of Aboriginal Title to water. However, it is, I believe, reasonable to assume that Aboriginal Title includes water. This principle is already well established south of the border, where, through what is called the Winters doctrine, US Tribes own water associated with their reservations. In the true reconciliation discussions that must inevitably ensue following the first title declaration in Canada, the question of the ownership of water will be an essential subject.

To date, in Canada, there has been no political recognition of Aboriginal Title to water. First Nations have often struggled to ensure fair access to water and have influence over its use by others – although there has been some recognition of the need to consult and accommodate First Nations interests when decisions affecting water allocation are made. In the modern treaties that have been negotiated in BC, the issue of First Nations access to water is addressed by the province creating a water reservation for the Nation. Governance of water in these treaties is addressed separately, both in terms of on settlement lands and in terms of involvement in decisions off settlement lands.

Interestingly, in 1909, when the province amended its land laws to exclude ownership of water, federal Indian Agents sought to acquire water rights for the reserves to be registered within the new provincial system. In this way, limited access to water for domestic and agricultural purposes on reserve was recorded. Today, notwithstanding Aboriginal Title to water, this is still the case for the most part and the way water rights for reserves are limited and recorded. However, some of our Nations simply exercise their Aboriginal Title to water by drawing from sources adjacent to or on their reserves, regardless of how other governments have determined how water is owned and controlled.

But it is important to appreciate that many of our Nations – through our teachings and our cultural beliefs – do not actually see natural resources, such as water, as commodities that can be owned in the Western sense. Rather, we are caretakers – resources are borrowed from future generations. In many of our cultures, we believe inanimate objects, including bodies of water, have their own identity and spirit – as a human does. Internationally, such Indigenous perspectives on the natural world are now beginning to influence environmental stewardship and in some cases are even reflected in legal codes – perhaps best encapsulated in the evolving legal concept of the rights of nature.

No doubt many of you are familiar with Ecuador's constitutional amendments of 2008, which provide rights for the natural world and were brought about by their Indigenous president, Rafael Correa. The Indigenous concept of *Buen Vivir* (or "good living") – which focuses on social, environmental, and spiritual wealth as opposed to material wealth – guided the new constitutional provisions, in which "nature" has fundamental and inalienable rights, reflecting the Indigenous belief that nature is the Mother and must be respected and, consequently, protected with legal standing.

As Indigenous Nations here in Canada rebuild, so, too, will our Nations develop laws that reflect differing perspectives on ownership, the environment, and the management and protection of natural resources. I would submit that these perspectives will help all of us to find the right balance between the need for exploiting natural resources to support economic growth and development with the need to ensure the preservation of the environment.

Turning to water governance from the perspective of the purveying of water from source to tap – the municipal side of water management – in BC, the provincial government establishes and regulates what entities can own and operate local water systems and sets the rules for how they are governed. The province also sets water-quality standards. On reserve, it is not so clear. The designing of governance structures, systems for water management, and the purveying of water is one of the many aspects of local government our peoples are grappling with. For bands that are not self-governing, the Indian Act still governs most aspects of reserve life. For water, as for most areas that need to be governed appropriately and effectively, the Indian Act provides very little guidance. While there are some bylaw-making powers for Chief and council – which some Nations have relied upon – these powers are limited, and there is nothing describing the governance structure for water. There are no legislated water-quality standards.

To fill this gap, Canada recently passed Bill S-8, the Safe Drinking Water for First Nations Act. The Act is not a recognition of self-government – there are no recognized law-making powers. The fundamental problem with this Act, like so many being developed by the Harper government, is that the bill was for the most part developed unilaterally by federal civil servants with limited consideration of First Nations perspectives. The Act contemplates that federal regulations will be developed for each province. There are serious questions about First Nations capacity, the cost of meeting the new rules, and building and maintaining infrastructure.

The impetus for this federal initiative was the continuing embarrassment of unsafe drinking water on so many reserves in Canada and the media attention this garners. There is no question that developing appropriate governance structures and standards for water quality on reserve is a shared objective, but with any reform comes the need for developing systems jointly and not simply transferring responsibility from one party to another. My hope is that First Nations will be able to address their governance more comprehensively and become self-governing and that the Act will not operate as a distraction from the larger objective – Nation rebuilding.

In addition to title to water and local governance, there is, of course, a whole other related conversation about industrial uses of water and water management, where water is used in processes such as fracking or where water quality is impacted by other industrial activities. With industrial water use, there are the same questions of ownership and jurisdiction but with an even greater need to address the environmental impacts and broader watershed management issues. How each of our Nations will be and are involved in governance on their title lands (including reserves and within their broader territory) or shared decision making with respect to industrial development is a live and ongoing issue.

Clearly, the movement to managing water based on watersheds as opposed to other geopolitical boundaries is the right way to go. It becomes more of a challenge where watersheds cross boundaries – whether international, between provinces or, indeed, intertribal. It is also complicated when multiple jurisdictions have concurrent authority regardless of boundary. As all governments – federal, provincial, and First Nation – are actively engaged in governance reform and updating their laws with respect to water, it is incumbent on all governments to coordinate and work together, to understand how our various governments with overlapping and concurrent jurisdiction will operate. Here in BC and, indeed, Canada, through our combined wisdom and efforts, we can set an example for the world when it comes to responsible and sustainable resource management.

On Certainty and Why It's Elusive

Address to the Business Council of British Columbia, April 13, 2018

A critical national conversation is taking place about reconciliation, the recognition and implementation of Indigenous Rights, and the place of Indigenous Peoples in decision making and governance in Canada. On February 14, 2018, in a historic address, Prime Minister Trudeau made a bold statement in the House of Commons, confirming that all relations with Indigenous Peoples are to be based on the recognition of Indigenous Rights and that a new Recognition and Implementation of Indigenous Rights Framework will be developed. And this work has now begun with a national engagement process.

Today, we are here together as part of that conversation. I expect that there are specific issues and topics on your mind. You want to understand how the work of reconciliation will lead to greater certainty and clarity for decision making and economic development. You want to understand how the recognition of rights relates to how projects will be approved and what processes will look like. You have questions about Indigenous consent and whether it will make things more or less challenging. I imagine some of you are also thinking about specific applications of these questions, including in light of the highly publicized and challenging issues of energy development, pipeline construction, and protection of our environment – or any other number of projects. Will the recognition and implementation of rights result in a future where the current realities of conflict, tension, cost, uncertainty, and litigation that we see embroiling some projects – and which no one desires – be changed or transformed for the better? You want to know how what we are doing today is different from what has been tried before.

It is true that in the past there have been attempts to reset the relationship with Indigenous Peoples, attempts at constitutional reform, legislative initiatives, and development of new policies, so what is different today?

What we are proposing is different: by coming from a rights-recognition perspective, the Government of Canada is finally being proactive and, in doing so, is not only transforming the status quo of how Canada operates and interacts with Indigenous Peoples but is also challenging, and supporting, Indigenous communities themselves – in a positive way – to lead change, rebuild, and find solutions and to take their rightful place within Confederation in ways that reflect Indigenous self-determination. And, if I can be so bold, had the approach we are taking today been the policy some thirty-six years ago, we might not be where we are today – that is, playing catch-up and trying to navigate the reactive politics that uncertainty breeds. It is precisely because rights have been denied, in the misplaced belief that it was prudent to do so, that we are here – seeking to undo decades of mistrust and begin, as we should have, on a solid foundation based on the recognition of rights.

So, let us dive in by addressing the issue of certainty. I think it is important to provide a definition of "certainty" at the outset, because it is so often used in different ways and means different things to different people in different contexts. "Certainty," for me, means clarity and predictability about the basic elements of decision making regarding lands and resources: who is making the decision, how the decisions are being made and through what process and timelines, what information and factors are relevant to the decision, and the respective roles and responsibilities of everyone involved. To say it another way, it is about clarity with respect to jurisdiction, law making, and authority.

Certainty, based on this definition, is something I think everyone desires – industry, Indigenous Peoples, and governments. However, currently, it does not exist enough. Where it does exist in some form, it is typically through agreements between the Crown and Indigenous Peoples, such as modern treaties and land claims agreements. And, there have been modern treaties – in fact over 40 percent of Canada's land mass, mostly in the North, is covered by modern treaties. But such agreements in BC have been few and far between, for reasons I will touch on later. And, of course, there is a long history of agreements such as historic treaties (which could provide some certainty) not being implemented or honoured.

Another circumstance where certainty, to a degree, sometimes exists has been when leadership has been shown by industry and Indigenous Peoples working together – forging relations and agreements about decision making and partnership regarding proposed projects. Certainty is also contributed to through initiatives like the Champions Table, a joint project of the Business Council of British Columbia and the BC Assembly of First Nations, where executives and Chiefs come together to develop common policy advice. But this can only go so far. Government, too, must act.

But beyond specific examples like these, for the most part we often live in a context of significant uncertainty. This is not good. And this is why we all have a stake in the ambitious agenda our government has set for reconciliation based on recognition, an agenda that must be nonpartisan and must survive beyond the life of any one government.

So why is certainty – which we all desire – so rare and elusive?

The answer lies in long-standing patterns and assumptions regarding Indigenous Rights, which, until we understand and transform them, will continue to be detrimental to Indigenous Peoples, Canadian society, and the economy as a whole. Let me explain. In Canada today, and ever since the adoption of section 35 of the Constitution in 1982, there has been a strong tendency to perceive and treat Indigenous Rights differently than other rights, such as Charter rights. When we think of or speak about freedom of expression, freedom of religion, or equality, I think it is fair to say we have a deep sense that these rights are part of what makes us uniquely Canadian. We do not question the existence of these rights – rather, we celebrate them. Without question, we view these rights as expressing an important aspect of who we are, our shared values, and what binds and defines us as a diverse and democratic society. While there always will be some disagreement on the margins about the precise scope or extent of these rights, they exist in the context of a broad consensus about what these rights definitely do mean and require. To say it another way, since 1982, when a Canadian says to its government, "I have a right to free speech under the Charter," the response of the Canadian government has not been to say, "Prove it." Rather, governments organize themselves – their laws, policies, and operational practices – to ensure they are upholding these rights.

Indigenous Rights, on the other hand, even though they were entrenched in section 35 of the Constitution at the same time as the Charter, have never, I would argue, been treated or thought of in the same way as Charter rights. Since 1982, when an Indigenous Nation raises a collective right under section 35, the response of governments has been to say, "Prove it." Despite section 35 saying that Indigenous Rights are "recognized and affirmed," successive governments have explicitly chosen to not recognize or affirm them – and, in so doing, have forced conflict and confusion about Indigenous Rights.

I would suggest that it is this choice – denial – that is at the heart of why we do not have certainty. Of course, this choice did not take place in a vacuum. It has been a long-standing pattern in Canadian history of denying Indigenous Peoples and their rights. This despite the fact the British Crown initially recognized Indigenous Peoples and their rights in the Royal Proclamation of 1763.

By the time of Confederation, in 1867, the fact that Indigenous Peoples had lived on and governed the lands and resources of their territories – something affirmed in the Royal Proclamation – was not considered. This denial has manifested itself throughout Canada's history, including through the passage and imposition of the Indian Act, the establishment of residential schools, efforts to eradicate Indigenous cultures and languages, the alienation of Indigenous Peoples from their homelands and territories, and the lack of implementation of treaties, or the failure to complete them altogether. And, of course, it has manifested itself in the positions the Crown has historically taken in court.

Critically important in this approach was the clear strategy by the Crown to divide up, and disempower, Indigenous Nations and governments. The goal was to remove and limit the capacity of Indigenous Nations to make decisions about their territories (as they had always done) in order to assimilate them. This was largely accomplished through creating and imposing an administrative reality that we are still confronting today – where, in the First Nations context, there are hundreds of Indian Act bands rather than dozens of linguistic and culturally structured Nations, meaning there are hundreds of groups (rather than dozens) representing peoples with historical and constitutionally protected rights and interests that often intersect, overlap, or interconnect with each other.

The uncertainty that we all experience today – Indigenous Peoples, industry, governments, and the Crown – whether what we witness is in relation to pipelines or any of a number of projects, has its roots directly in this history of denial and division. Moving forward, this has critical implications for reconciliation. It means Indigenous Nations – the proper title and rights holders – because of colonial imposition, may not be operating with political, economic, and social structures or the resources necessary to fully discharge their responsibilities as caretakers of their lands or a context for clear Indigenous governance, law making, and decision making. The entrenchment of Aboriginal and Treaty Rights in section 35 of the Constitution was supposed to break this pattern. However, the maintenance of a "prove it" approach by governments after 1982 made success in transforming relations extremely difficult.

We experience the effects of this denial every day. It is at the root of the conflict and ever increasing complexity about decision making. It plagues agreement making and treaty implementation because often-untenable positions are advanced. It explains why we have so much litigation, where instead of developing a shared understanding of rights we turned to the courts as the central institution of Crown-Indigenous relations. It has delayed the critical work of Nation building and rebuilding, which is necessary so Indigenous Peoples can take back control of their own affairs, make their own decisions, and be, once again, responsible for their own future. Rather than investing as much as we could have in the institutions, processes, and capacity development needed for rebuilding Indigenous Nations and governments and ultimately improving the lives of Indigenous Peoples, we have all spent far too much of our limited resources and energy on conflict.

The costs of denial have been immense.

As an Indigenous woman, I know the effect of these choices directly and intimately. They have perpetuated the impoverishment and marginalization of Indigenous Peoples from Canadian society – with massive impacts on both individual lives and collective Indigenous well-being. But they have also been negative for Canada as a whole – socially, economically, and culturally – including in how they have influenced our investment climate, efforts at environmental protection, and regulation of lands and resources.

So what does it take to actually build certainty? It requires that we finally address the impediments to increased certainty by overturning its root cause – the denial of rights. This is one thing that the recognition-of-rights approach that our government has committed to will help accomplish. Through the Recognition and Implementation of Indigenous Rights Framework, the work of government will shift from processes primarily focused on assessing whether rights exist – which, inevitably, is adversarial and contentious – to seeking shared understandings about how the priorities and rights of Indigenous Peoples may be implemented and expressed within a particular process and its outcome. This shift – supported by legislative measures that help build trust that government will act according to certain transparent standards – will help create opportunities for collaboration and reduce the intensity of conflict. This shift will also include a movement away from reliance upon and use of the courts. Not only will there be less incentives to fight, there will also be new opportunities to avoid fighting when conflict may arise.

For example, I will shortly be releasing a new litigation directive to my department regarding section 35 rights. While there will be many details of the directive worth exploring in the future – its overall orientation is most critical. It will aim to reposition Canada's legal approach to being problem solvers on the path of reconciliation, with the courts as a last resort, to be turned to only in increasingly rare circumstances. This means the refocusing of lawyers and their ways of thinking and stronger investments in preventing and proactively resolving matters before they reach the stage of litigation. To this end, a significant emphasis will also be placed on new dispute-resolution and accountability mechanisms that will help resolve matters outside of the courts.

A recognition-of-rights approach also includes abandoning old positions that were the main barriers to reaching broad understandings and arrangements with Indigenous Peoples about how rights will be respected and implemented collaboratively. For example, Canada is abandoning its position that treaties, agreements, and other constructive arrangements must include the extinguishment, modification, or surrender of rights – a position that has resulted in negotiations being interminably slow or never beginning in the first place. The result of this shift is already being felt as Canada is now rapidly accelerating tables with dozens of communities and Nations based on the recognition of rights.

Perhaps most importantly, however, a shift to recognition of rights, including Indigenous self-determination and the inherent right of self-government, means that Canada will be an active supporter in the building and rebuilding of Indigenous Nations and governments. We will finally be active partners in supporting Indigenous Nations and governments as they do the work of defining and clarifying their constitutions, laws, and decision-making processes, the structures they will work through, and how they will govern as part of historic rights-bearing groups, including those with historic treaties. We will also finally be partners in building with those Indigenous governments the proper intergovernmental arrangements that allow everyone to have clarity and certainty about the "who," "how," and "what" of land and resource decision making. In short, we will support Nation building and rebuilding so we know who speaks for the Nation and that when the Nation does speak their voice can be relied upon.

We have already begun to reflect this approach in Bill C-69, which deals with major project reviews and impact assessment, where the legislation contemplates an increased role for Indigenous Peoples in decision making with a placeholder for what is contemplated to be forthcoming in light of the more fulsome rights-recognition framework with self-governing reconstituted nations. As this legislation goes through the Parliamentary process, and is implemented, it will be informed by the Recognition and Implementation of Indigenous Rights Framework as we continue to work with Indigenous Peoples, industry, and all Canadians, to ensure we implement new processes that build regulatory certainty and predictability, recognize and respect the right of Indigenous Peoples, as well as protecting the environment for generations to come.

To be clear then, this work of recognition is very much two-pronged. There was and is significant work to do for Canada to get its house in order. There is also significant work for Indigenous Peoples to do. We are in a period of transition, and, as I said at the outset, we are challenging the status quo. This work involves Nations, based on their right to self-determination, rebuilding and reconstituting themselves, including for First Nations rebuilding their own political, social, and economic structures and moving beyond the Indian Act, as they determine. This is work only Indigenous Peoples, Nations, and governments can lead and do. They must make the hard choices of how they want to structure and govern themselves as Nations and governments today as well as determine the laws and processes they will apply for decisions to be made.

Government must support Indigenous Nations in this work – to thrive and be effective in making decisions and caring for the well-being of their citizens. This will mean new mechanisms and tools that support their effectiveness, including a new fiscal relationship with the government.

I hope this gives you a clear vision of how I view certainty and how the Recognition and Implementation of Indigenous Rights Framework will advance certainty. By moving from denial to recognition – by embracing this transition – we also move from uncertainty to clarity and predictability.

This brings me to the second and related topic – that of free, prior, and informed consent and, more generally, the role of Indigenous Peoples in decision making. I think too often "consent" is used as a rhetorical device in the context of potential conflict or for political purposes, while too rarely do we actually have a discussion about how to pragmatically operationalize and implement it. I think consent requires a bit of demystification, as well as some straight talk.

I have three observations to share.

First, we need to be clear that the issue of consent is not a "new" one, an idea that has somehow arisen because of the United Nations Declaration. Consent has been noted as a matter to be addressed in Crown-Indigenous relations by the courts for many years in the interpretation of section 35, including in cases such as *Delgamuukw* (1997), *Haida* (2004), and *Tsilhqot'in* (2014). Indeed, in *Tsilhqot'in*, the court, in paragraph 97, recommended and encouraged shifting to "obtaining consent" as the standard for governments and industry in relations with Indigenous Peoples, regardless of whether court declarations or findings had been issued. The rationale for doing this is that it would remove the likelihood of conflict, legal struggles, and uncertainty about a project or decision. Moreover, even though we have tended to use different language, de facto consent is something that both governments and industry have, over the years, sometimes realized is necessarily part of the path forward. This is one of the underlying reasons for many of the "impact and benefit agreements" that industry has properly pursued.

Second, we have tended to think about consent through the lens of the processes we currently used for consultation and accommodation and that somehow consent involves doing what we have already been doing, with additional enhancements involving whether or not consent is achieved. I would suggest that this is not a very helpful way of thinking about consent. Consent is not simply an extension of existing processes of consultation and accommodation, nor is the law of consultation – being heavily procedural in its orientation – a particularly practical or helpful way for thinking about how to operationalize consent. We need to see consent as part and parcel of the new relationship we are seeking to build with Indigenous Nations, as proper title and rights holders, who are reconstituting and rebuilding their political, economic, and social structures.

In this context, there is a better way to think about consent, one that is grounded in the purposes and goals of section 35 and the UN Declaration. Consent is analogous to the types of relations we typically see, and are familiar with, between governments. In such relations, where governments must work together, there are a range of mechanisms that are used to ensure that the authority and autonomy of both governments is respected and that decisions are made in a way that is consistent and coherent and does not often lead to regular or substantial disagreement. These mechanisms are diverse and can range from shared bodies and structures, to utilizing the same information and standards, to agreeing on long-term plans or arrangements that will give clarity on how all decisions will be made on a certain matter or in a certain area over time. Enacting these mechanisms is achieved through a multiplicity of tools – including legislation, policy, and agreements.

The structures and mechanisms for achieving this consent, once established, are also consistent over time and across types of decisions (they are known and transparent), roles and responsibilities are defined, and they are ready to be implemented when needed. One result of this is significant certainty.

So coming back to where I began my comments, consider for a moment what would have happened if we had spent even a little time over the last thirty-five years (since section 35 came into being) building those structures – including undertaking and supporting Indigenous Nation rebuilding – rather than endlessly litigating. I think we would be in a totally different place than what we are witnessing now regarding the challenges we see in project development, economic growth, and environmental protection. I see our work of moving towards consent-based decision making as building these structures and mechanisms of consistent, collaborative decision making with Indigenous Nations.

The recognition-of-rights framework we are working towards in partnership with Indigenous Peoples is intended to create the legislative and policy space to do this work, and also accelerate it so that we are not waiting another generation for this work to be substantially advanced. We cannot wait. Through the engagement process, we are hearing, amongst other things, about the need for recognition legislation, the need for new institutions and supports for Indigenous Nation building, new accountability and oversight mechanisms, and new forms of dispute resolution. The proposed rights-recognition framework should not prescribe or define a new way of consulting and accommodating, or of obtaining consent, but rather should focus on establishing legislative space and standards as well as investments in the work of building effective relations between the federal government and Indigenous governments, including around how decisions are made.

Third, this understanding of consent also clarifies that for consent to be fully operationalized as part of a relationship between governments, significant work has to be done by Indigenous Nations, in addition to the federal or provincial governments. In particular, Indigenous Nations need to do work to reconstitute their Nations and governments in ways consistent with the principles in domestic law around the proper rights holder and understandings of Indigenous Peoples at international law. This is part of Indigenous Peoples ensuring that Indigenous jurisdiction and authority, including the giving of consent, are being properly granted and exercised consistent with the right to self-determination. One implication of this is that consent will not be operationalized in a linear or uniform manner. It will occur in a diversity of ways, with various steps and stages being taken in different contexts and relationships at different times.

There will inevitably be critics of this work. Some of it will come from Indigenous leadership. There were those who did not support section 35, and there were those who do not like the United Nations Declaration. But – and this is where I speak to you not as the Minister of Justice and Attorney General of Canada but as a former Regional Chief, a former councillor in my community, and a proud Indigenous person – I know that for the vast majority of Indigenous leaders, past and present, this has been what people have been saying needs to be done for years. These are not new ideas. They are not necessarily my ideas. So as my colleague Minister Bennett goes out and "consults" – please keep this in mind. This caution is because the changes we are pursuing through the framework have the potential to uproot long-standing obstacles and attitudes – from all quarters – that have held back Indigenous Peoples and all of Canadian society, including industry.

Uncertainty, conflict, and endless litigation are not the result of trying to do the right thing – they are the result of trying to avoid doing the right thing for whatever political motivation. The promise of section 35 of our Constitution is rights recognition. It is through rights recognition that we will build patterns of effective and strong Indigenous governments that

Restoring Balance,
Correcting Injustices,
and Keeping Vigilant

"

Empowering women and girls
empowers humanity.

"

"

Canada's justice system has
historically had a role in perpetuating injustice
for Indigenous Peoples.

"

A Litmus Test for Reconciliation
Is the Status of Women

Opening Remarks, "Raising the Bar: Indigenous Women's Impact
on the Law-Scape," Public Policy Forum, October 30, 2018

Indigenous women have had experiences of the Canadian legal order like no other peoples – including that of being invisible. Throughout Canada's history, in various ways, Indigenous women have not been seen by the Canadian legal order. Sometimes, this invisibility has been express, including not having basic political, legal, or economic rights. This has included being deprived of some of those rights that have been held by Indigenous men or non-Indigenous women. Sometimes, including more recently, this invisibility has been through how our legal order perceives, treats, and responds to the actions, claims, and realities of Indigenous women and girls – including experiences of violence.

There are many forces and factors that have contributed to this invisibility. A powerful one has been the effects of colonialism on Indigenous legal orders. This denial has resulted in an erosion of roles, responsibilities, and authorities for Indigenous women. It has contributed to the specific forms of marginalization and disempowerment that Indigenous women continue to confront and has affected ways of thinking about women as legal actors and agents.

I know this from my own reality. I come from a matrilineal society with hereditary Chiefs. Being matrilineal means that descent is traced through the mother and our maternal ancestors. Power and inheritance flow through the mother's line. For me, this was typified by my grandmother, Pugladee, which is the highest-ranking name in our Clan. Her name means "a good host" – a name that was given to my older sister, Kory. My name, Puglaas, means "a woman born to noble people." The names were given in a naming Potlatch when I was five and my sister six.

In my peoples' worldview, which animates our laws and legal order, all things are in their greatest state of well-being when there is balance. This includes balance between humans and the natural world, between genders, between groups of peoples, within a family or community, or in how we live and organize our own lives. Balance is viewed as the proper state of things, where conditions of harmony and justice flourish, while imbalance is what gives rise to conflict, contention, and harm. In this worldview, if women are not playing their needed roles in leadership, in law, in family – in all aspects of society – then there is an imbalance, and all suffer. A society imbalanced in this way is like a bird with an injured wing. It cannot fly, its purpose and potential cannot be met, and all are held back.

But the reality since colonization has been that the matrilineal political and legal order of which I am a part as an Indigenous woman – and which has been in place since time immemorial – has been largely incomprehensible to the Canadian legal order. The Indian Act system imposed on my peoples, like other Indigenous Peoples across the country, is based on a different legal order – or tradition – that is totally foreign to the roles of women, balance, integration, and harmony that my ancestors had lived according to for countless generations. It imported a patriarchal system with an understanding of law rooted in force, power, and control – and which the majority of Indigenous Peoples across this country continue to bear the burdens of today.

This is why when we talk about building the future, as we all do – a future of reconciliation, of nation-to-nation relationships – I see a fundamental litmus test of progress being around the topics you are discussing tonight. Because any meaningful effort to address our colonial reality must revolve around Indigenous Peoples determining their futures, including rebuilding their Nations and governments and their legal orders and jurisdictions in the contemporary world. And a measure of success in Nations doing this work will be if the roles, responsibilities, and authorities of women in the political, social, and legal work of their Nations and the well-being of Indigenous women and girls in Canadian society as a whole are steadily increased. If this is not occurring, then the work of self-determination, and the work of transforming our colonial reality, is not being advanced and achieved – as it surely must.

Building this future means accepting that Canada has always been a country of legal pluralism – the coming together of different legal orders that learn to coexist and operate together. This was true at the founding of the country 150 years ago in relation to our common law and civil law heritage. At that time, the Indigenous legal orders were ignored, and repairing that is core to the work we are doing today. While Indigenous Peoples must lead this work, the Crown has a responsibility to affirm the appropriate space for the operation and application of Indigenous laws and legal orders through changes to our own existing laws – including getting rid of the Indian Act – and creating new models of relations. This requires moving beyond the practice of denying the operation of Indigenous laws and legal orders and creating patterns of legal pluralism that recognize them and include their roles.

Let me be clear, there is little or no chance for Indigenous legal traditions to find their full expression within our system of multilevel governance in Canada while the Indian Act remains so prevalent. The Indian Act is the antithesis of self-government as an expression of self-determination and, moreover, is an ongoing detriment to Nation rebuilding and strong and appropriate Indigenous governance. We must all stop trying to make the round peg of the Indian Act fit into the square hole of Indigenous Rights and then somehow think we can rely on the courts to figure it all out. Rather, we must recognize the plurality of legal traditions in this country and, in so doing, create the space for Indigenous Nation rebuilding as part of our evolving system of cooperative federalism.

Now, I should say that I do believe important progress is being made, and Indigenous women are taking a leadership role. In my experience, it is typically the women in our communities who are leading the charge to decolonize and rebuild our governance models as our Nations move away from colonial systems. It is the work I was doing before I moved into my current role, a role I take incredibly seriously, although at times it can be a challenge and incredibly frustrating. Indeed, in my own experience serving as the first Indigenous person to be Canada's Minister of Justice and Attorney General, I have unfortunately had it reinforced that when addressing Indigenous issues, no matter what table one sits around, or in what position, or with what title and appearance of influence and power, the experience of marginalization can still carry with you. But this does not deter me. It only makes my resolve stronger and more determined, as I believe that our toil today is not only helping create the pivotal space and opportunity for Nation rebuilding but also creating the space for the countless Indigenous girls who will fill leadership roles today and many others in the future, in contexts ever more receptive and supportive of their talents, capacities, and remarkable contributions to the well-being of our society, country, and world.

My belief that progress is being made and that the fruits of the sacrifices of today will often appear more concrete tomorrow – this is what assists me in carrying on, despite the obstacles, this and my deeply rooted sense of who I am, where I come from, my teachings – my rights and responsibilities. So while there remains much work to be done – and the work goes on – events like tonight remind me of why we are doing it, what must be done, and that it is in our shared efforts and the contributions that each of us can make that the pathways of change are being laid.

Preventing First Contacts
with the Criminal Justice System

Adapted from "Recognition, Reconciliation,
and Indigenous People's Disproportionate Interactions with the Justice System,"
Inaugural Houston Lecture, Johnson Shoyama Graduate School of Public Policy,
University of Saskatchewan, September 13, 2018

I worked as a prosecutor in Vancouver's Downtown Eastside before turning my focus specifically to Indigenous Rights. My upbringing, my education, and my professional and personal experiences have all shaped my worldview and strengthened my determination to see a genuine transformation in Canada's relationship with Indigenous Peoples and to be a part of meaningful and lasting improvements to the criminal justice system. In doing this work, I was and am building upon the advocacy and leadership of generations of Indigenous Elders, leaders, and people who have come before me, including my father. They devoted their lives to ensuring their way of life, their culture, their systems of governments and laws, their connection with lands and resources, and their economic opportunities could be maintained and improved upon.

As a proud Indigenous woman, with the great responsibility of being Canada's first ever Indigenous Minister of Justice and Attorney General, I feel a moral imperative to carry on this work and to help advance the necessary shifts that need to take place. I see my appointment to this role not so much as a personal accomplishment but rather as a symbol of how far Canada has come – but also how much further we have to go. So I would like to address two very important and interrelated topics: the rebuilding of Indigenous Nations and governments in Canada and how modernizing the Canadian criminal justice system will help address the disproportionate number of interactions that Indigenous People experience with it.

In Canada, the federal government has sole jurisdiction over criminal law, although the administration of justice is a shared responsibility among federal, provincial, and territorial governments. Throughout our history, there have been serious and lasting implications for Indigenous Peoples as a result of how this arrangement, and the administration of justice, has evolved and been operationalized. Indeed, the impacts of our justice system on Indigenous People have been front and centre in our public discourses over the past number of years – including, certainly, very directly in this province. Painful and tragic realities and experiences have been starkly revealed, long-standing concerns with the administration of justice have had a light shone on them, and Canadians from coast to coast to coast have begun to understand in new and renewed ways the histories and legacies that have led to these enduring challenges, and the directions of change we must pursue.

There remains significant unfinished work to accomplish before Indigenous Peoples have access to appropriate systems of justice, including Indigenous courts, so that they can enforce tribal and other laws as part of our multilevel system of evolving cooperative federalism. The work involved in rebuilding Indigenous systems of justice is part of the broader work of Indigenous Nation rebuilding and finding ways to overcome the long and tragic history of the colonization of Indigenous Peoples in Canada. Reconciliation with Indigenous Peoples – which must be rooted in real and fulsome recognition, affirmation, and implementation of the inherent rights of Indigenous Peoples, in ways that reflect how Indigenous Peoples have understood those words and terms over generations – remains one of the most urgent and compelling issues facing Canadians today, and reforms to the criminal justice system represent an important, even vital, step in the path towards reconciliation.

Before turning to the criminal justice system specifically, first let me say a few comments about the era of reconciliation that we are in. And let me tell you of my understanding of what is involved in successfully navigating the path towards reconciliation. At the heart of achieving reconciliation is the belief that the nation-to-nation, government-to-government,

Inuit-Crown relationship must be based on the recognition of rights, respect, cooperation, and partnership.

So let me pause for a second on this term "recognition of rights." Words have meaning. We live in a time where language is often appropriated and misused, co-opted and twisted – made to stand for something it is not. "Recognition" for Indigenous Peoples across this country, and as a basis for true reconciliation, has meaning. It means that Indigenous Peoples governed and owned the lands that now make up Canada prior to the arrival of Europeans. It means that Indigenous laws and legal orders that stewarded the lands for millennia remain and must continue to operate in the contemporary world. It means that the title and rights of Indigenous Peoples are inherent and not dependent or contingent on court orders, agreements, or government action for their existence, substance, and effect. It means that treaties entered into historically must be fully implemented based on their spirit and intent, oral histories as well as texts, and consistent with the true meaning of a proper nation-to-nation and government-to-government relationship. It means that the distinct and diverse governments, laws, cultures, societies, and ways of life of First Nations, Métis, and Inuit are fully respected and reflected.

For Canada, recognition means resetting our foundation to properly reconcile – to finish the unfinished business of Confederation. What is more, for many Indigenous Peoples, recognition is the lifeline that will ensure the survival and rebuilding of their cultures, languages, and governing systems within an even stronger Canada.

But words are also easy and cheap. And too often we see the tendency – especially in politics – to use important words that have real meaning and importance carelessly. We see them being applied to ideas and actions that in truth do not reflect their actual meaning – even, sometimes, their opposite. We see "recognition" applied to ideas that actually maintain "denial." We see "self-government" used to refer to ideas or processes that actually maintain control over others. We see "self-determination" applied to actions that actually interfere with the work of Nations rebuilding their governments and communities. We see "inherent" in the same breath as the contradictory idea that rights are contingent on the courts or agreements.

When we see this being done, it does not advance reconciliation. It actually undermines it. It causes confusion, chaos, and division. It treats a challenge – a challenge that is vital for the survival and well-being of children, women, families, and communities across this country – as a "game of rhetoric." It trivializes – often out of ignorance or political expediency – a moral, social, and economic imperative for our country. Words, in the work of reconciliation, are also cheap without real action, action that goes to the core of undoing the colonial laws, policies, and practices and that is based on the real meaning of reconciliation. We all need to understand this. The path of justice and equality is not advanced or achieved through half-measures, good intentions, or lofty rhetoric. And it is certainly not achieved through obfuscation or confusion about what we mean when we speak. Hard choices, innovative actions, transformations in laws and policies, new understandings and attitudes, new patterns of behaviour – this is what is needed.

As Minister of Justice and one whose life-long commitment has been to the recognition of rights, my message has always been consistent and considered – both internally and externally – that transformative change requires a coherent and comprehensive approach to the true recognition of the inherent rights of Indigenous Peoples. This work is incredibly hard but must continue. I will carry on with my advocacy for the necessary transformative actions that will create the space – the foundation – for self-determination and the rebuilding of Indigenous Nations within Canada. We all need to be advocates in this work.

So, while I have been thrilled in recent years to see how Canadians – and governments – have begun to "talk the talk" of reconciliation, I remain constantly, incessantly, vigilant in demanding that we honour the meaning of these important words and that words translate into real, transformative action. We all need to remain vigilant in that regard if we actually want to see the justice and equality in Canada that we have been striving towards. For my part, and to be very candid, I have been challenged, but I also challenge constantly. And I will continue to do that every day I have the privilege to be the Minister of Justice and Attorney General of Canada. With that in mind, my focus on reconciliation, and in supporting the work involved in rebuilding Indigenous Nations, as I said from the outset, is both personal and professional.

In the spirit of Nations rebuilding, how does making foundational changes based on the recognition of rights relate to Indigenous People in the criminal justice system and the modernization of Canada's criminal justice system? Today, Indigenous People are overrepresented in our criminal justice system, as both victims and offenders. We are far more likely than any other Canadian to be victims of crime and homicide and are far more likely to be arrested, prosecuted, and incarcerated. For example, Indigenous People suffer a homicide rate that is nearly seven times higher than that of non-Indigenous Canadians. According to the most recent statistics, the rate of violent victimization among Indigenous People in Canada is more than double that of non-Indigenous people. Worse yet, Indigenous identity appears to be a risk factor for the violent victimization of Indigenous women. The overall rate of violent victimization among Indigenous women was double that of Indigenous men and close to triple that of non-Indigenous women.

According to Statistics Canada, Indigenous adults comprised 4 percent of Canada's population but represented 27 percent of admissions to federal custody and 30 percent in provincial and territorial custody. In Saskatchewan, that number is a staggering 76 percent. In 2015–16, despite representing approximately 5 percent of Canada's total female population, Indigenous women made up 38 percent of the federally incarcerated female population in Canada. In 2016–17, in one rather staggering statistic, Indigenous women made up 85 percent of women in custody in Saskatchewan. In 2016–17, Indigenous youth accounted for 46 percent of admissions to correctional services while representing just 8 percent of the Canadian youth population.

All these figures, and the tragic reality they help illustrate, are, of course, completely unacceptable and must change. As a former prosecutor, this story is all too familiar to me. A young person, often an Indigenous man, commits a nonviolent crime, comes into contact with the criminal justice system and never is really able to pull himself free. He gets caught in a vicious cycle of court appearances, court orders, breaches of court orders, and returns to custody. Soon, he is spending more time behind bars than he is out of them. This man's interactions with the criminal justice system have further marginalized him, making him even more vulnerable.

We need to find better ways of preventing Indigenous People from experiencing that first contact with the criminal justice system. And for those already in the system, we need to better support them when they leave it. This could mean more treatment for addictions or mental health issues or more services aimed at helping to find housing, employment, and educational opportunities. To be successful, we first must acknowledge and act on the understanding that the current circumstances faced by Indigenous People in the criminal justice system are inseparable from the historic and contemporary impacts of colonialism and the denial of Indigenous Rights. It is in such a context that disempowerment, hopelessness, cycles of violence, and desperation grow. It is also in that context that a criminal justice system has emerged with structures, patterns, and norms that are often alienating, unresponsive, and not culturally relevant.

That is why the work of supporting the recognition and implementation of Indigenous Rights, including Indigenous self-determination and the inherent right of self-government, is so critical to establishing a foundation where current and future generations of Indigenous youth are born and raised in conditions that see that their well-being and ability to thrive will continually increase, where they have hope and where their interactions with the criminal justice system continually decrease. The work to accomplish this will include supporting Indigenous self-governments in developing their own systems for the administration of justice while also reforming the current systems of justice that fall under the jurisdictions of federal and provincial governments.

To facilitate this work, I believe we must bring together Indigenous Nations, leaders, experts, and stakeholders in rebuilding Indigenous systems of justice as part of the broader and ongoing Nation rebuilding work. This is something that I am committed to doing in the next year, including for those Indigenous governments that are already self-governing but may not have yet been able to establish an effective judicial system. This is a justice endeavour that I am passionate about and one that possibly some of you, or this institution, may also be interested in or could assist with. It will necessarily include provincial and federal officials who, in many cases, are responsible for enforcing and adjudicating tribal laws in the absence of a tribal court.

As we strive to reform the systems of justice and support Indigenous Nation rebuilding, we must also increase or introduce measures and initiatives within the current justice system aimed at reducing the likelihood of an Indigenous person being at disproportionate risk of getting caught in a continuous cycle of interactions with the criminal justice system. Fortunately, our government has already begun to deliver on five ongoing initiatives that I am very hopeful about.

The first initiative is expanding the use of restorative justice, which emphasizes repairing the relationship between the victim and the offender. Restorative justice is focused more on collaboration and inclusivity and is often more culturally relevant and responsive to specific communities. Victims have a powerful voice, and this process allows them to be heard and to heal, while at the same time holding the offender accountable for their actions. In this sense, I sometimes view restorative justice as acting as a kind of circuit breaker from the cycle that so many find themselves caught in. While restorative justice has been part of Canada's criminal justice system for over forty years and has proven effective over that period, it is still not widely available across the country. A 2011 Department of Justice Canada report found that Indigenous People who completed a community-based alternative to mainstream justice, such as restorative justice, were significantly less likely to reoffend than those who did not. I am committed to expanding this resource so it can be more widely used and accepted across the country.

A second initiative is through Indigenous-specific sentencing courts in the existing provincial justice system, which focus on community reintegration and healing. We are also beginning to see courts established by Indigenous governments emerging in the context of self-government, although, at this point, they are not dealing with criminal matters.

Measures such as specialized courts and restorative justice are aimed at solving the problem that caused the behaviour in the first place, as opposed to strictly placing the primary focus on punishment. This provides offenders, where appropriate, with a way out of the system. While I strongly believe that offenders must be held to account for their actions, I also believe that the system must be fair for all those who come before it. The right reforms will bring us closer to both goals simultaneously. This is not an either-or proposition.

Another initiative is one aimed at addressing the overincarceration of Indigenous People for administration of justice offences, such as bail breaches, which can further compound the tragic cycle of incarceration. Earlier this year, I introduced Bill C-75, major legislation to address delays in the criminal justice system that includes changes to how bail is granted and to how breaches of bail conditions will be administered. Accused who do not have access to needed supports and services – such as housing, health care, and social services – are at a higher risk of breaching bail conditions. This can result in further needless incarceration while awaiting trial, which further contributes to the overrepresentation of Indigenous People and vulnerable persons in the criminal justice system.

There are also proposed changes to how juries are selected. While Indigenous People are overrepresented as victims and offenders, they are underrepresented on juries. We continue to work towards a jury selection system that better represents our Nation's diversity and that enjoys the confidence of all Canadians.

In addition to these initiatives, our government has also introduced a more transparent and open process for choosing federally appointed judges, with a focus on promoting a modern bench that better reflects Canada's diversity. I have made it a priority of mine to ensure that Indigenous People, women, and marginalized communities are better represented on the bench. Judicial diversity refers to both gender diversity, which ensures that more women are appointed to the bench, and individual diversity, which aims to capture the diversity of our multicultural population. We believe that a diverse judicial bench allows those who come before the criminal justice system, either as victims or accused, to see themselves better represented in the system, which helps build confidence in our institutions. Judicial appointees' diversity, in both professional and life experience, along with their ties to the community in which they sit, are critical to ensuring that judicial benches reflect, and receive, the respect of the communities they serve. We have also reformed how justices of the Supreme Court of Canada are selected. A potential consideration for candidates now includes their knowledge of Indigenous legal traditions. While there is currently no Indigenous person on the Supreme Court, I can certainly foresee that historic day coming.

In conclusion, I absolutely do not want to imply that our criminal justice system has been fixed, far from it. However, we find ourselves in a period of significant change. While considerable progress has been made, our justice system remains a living testament to many of the discriminatory policies and practices of our past, a past which continues to negatively impact Indigenous People and communities as well as vulnerable populations across Canada. Addressing the overpolicing and overincarceration of Indigenous Peoples in this country will not happen overnight. By being vigilant, honouring the sacrifices of generations of Indigenous Peoples who have been fighting for justice in the face of colonialism, and reshaping laws and policies based on the real meaning of recognition of rights, we will effect a fundamental and positive change in the relationship between Indigenous Peoples and the criminal justice system. We all have a role to play.

On Sticking Our Necks Out

Address to the BC Cabinet and First Nations Leaders' Gathering,
November 29, 2018

When I spoke at this gathering in 2014, on behalf of the Chiefs, I advanced our "Four Principles." The "Four Principles" were developed by consensus of the Chiefs of British Columbia as we came together in 2014 – both those groups involved in the BC treaty-making process and those seeking recognition of rights outside of that process. The principles stated the requisites for true nation-to-nation and government-to-government relationships consistent with the recognition of rights, Indigenous self-determination, the inherent right of self-government, and the necessary roles for Indigenous laws and jurisdictions. That meeting was in the shadow of the *Tsilhqot'in* (2014) decision of the Supreme Court of Canada, and there was a clear sense that momentum towards change was building.

Later, when I was here speaking on behalf of the Government of Canada, the underlying message was the same, and I stressed how forming relations based on the recognition and implementation of rights is now the shared work of all of us, including non-Indigenous governments needing to make legislative, policy, and practice changes. I again spoke of the "Four Principles," this time as a minister of the Crown. I also spoke about how Indigenous Peoples must lead the way, and the hard questions that you – we – as Indigenous Peoples must answer. And I want to reiterate those sentiments today. Indigenous self-determination requires that we –

Indigenous Peoples – do the work of rebuilding our Nations and our governments, work that no one can do, prescribe, or dictate for us. For proper nation-to-nation and government-to-government relations to emerge, we must revitalize our Indigenous laws, governments, and jurisdictions and be organized as proper title and rights holders.

Today, my underlying message is the same, but my remarks will be a little different. I think it is timely to share with you some reflections that are in my mind and heart about what we have seen transpire in recent months. To take stock, so to speak, about where we are at in this vital work and where we may go next. "The time is always right to do what is right." These words by Martin Luther King Jr. evoke a truth that Indigenous Peoples in this country know all too well. The work that needs to be done is urgent – and it has been urgent for generations. There have always been excuses for delay and inaction. We know them well. We often hear "It is hard," "It is complicated," "We don't understand."

But the reality is that we know what must be done. We have the solutions. Indigenous Peoples have articulated what needs to happen for decades. Studies and reports have laid out paths forward, including comprehensively in the Royal Commission on Aboriginal Peoples and the calls to action of the Truth and Reconciliation Commission. We have hundreds of court cases about section 35 of the Constitution and a global consensus around the standards for survival, dignity, and well-being of Indigenous Peoples in the United Nations Declaration on the Rights of Indigenous Peoples.

The common theme in the solutions provided is the necessity to shift from the denial of rights to their recognition and implementation, including Indigenous self-determination and the inherent right of self-government. The inhumane conditions and suffering that Indigenous Peoples have and continue to experience are rooted in legislation, policies, and practices that did not treat Indigenous People as fully equal, autonomous human beings with dignity, rights, and respect. The imposition of the Indian Act on the lives of Indigenous Peoples, the breaking up of our governments and Nations, the lack of implementation of treaties, failing to embrace the standards in section 35 of the Constitution and the United Nations Declaration on the Rights of Indigenous Peoples – these forms of denial are the foundation of our current challenges.

We will never comprehensively solve the massive rates of our children in care, the ravages of the drug epidemic in our communities, the tragedy of youth suicide, and other major challenges we confront everyday unless and until the authority, capacity, and responsibility of Indigenous Nations and their governments to determine their futures and care for their peoples are affirmed and implemented.

I have described the work that the Government of Canada is undertaking with respect to Indigenous issues as moving on two interdependent tracks. The first track is closing-the-gap issues – ensuring potable water, access to quality education, addressing issues of children and family and the unacceptable rate of kids in care. The second track is the foundation and transformational piece – rights recognition. This track is making the transformative changes to laws, policies, and practices and doing the work of Nation and government rebuilding by replacing denial with recognition as the foundation of our relations. Both tracks are needed – interrelated – and the first will never be fully realized, the gaps closed, until and unless the second is made real. Thinking that good intentions, tinkering around the edges of the Indian Act, or making increased financial investments (however significant and unprecedented) will in themselves close the gaps is naive. Transformative change and new directions are required.

Maybe think of it through the analogy of a tree. As we all know, if the roots of a tree are dead, the tree will not grow, even if we water it. And while the trunk may stand for years, at some point it falls over and begins rotting. For too long, our main strategy has been to pour water on dead roots, hoping that the tree will grow. Of course, it does not.

What we need to do together, Crown governments and Indigenous Peoples, and this work is long overdue, is dig up the dead roots and plant something new and then properly water and fertilize it. Entrenching the recognition of rights in federal and provincial laws, policies, and practices – if done properly, in a way that recognizes the legitimate polities of Indigenous Peoples – is the soil for the new healthy roots of strong and rebuilt postcolonial Indigenous Nations and in which our collective and shared future will grow. A new tree.

But I think we all know this. Yet, regrettably, it still has not happened in any comprehensive way. We need to continue to ask ourselves why and to challenge ourselves to confront that which stands in the way, wherever the obstacles are coming from – be it from within government or outside. The answer to overcoming the obstacles is having the necessary collective political will to reset the relationship based on the recognition and implementation of rights.

For three years, within government and publicly, I have been explicit in outlining what I see as minimum elements of new relations based on the recognition of rights – a rights-recognition framework – elements that are what Indigenous Peoples have advocated for over generations. They include

- harmony between the laws of Canada and UNDRIP
- the replacement of the Comprehensive Land Claims Policy, the Inherent Right of Self-Government Policy, and consultation and accommodation approaches with policies based on true recognition
- legislated, binding standards on all public officials to ensure they act in all matters with Indigenous Peoples based on recognition of title and rights
- legislative, binding obligations on the Crown to take action in partnership with Indigenous Nations to implement models of self-government that are self-determined by Indigenous Peoples
- accountable, independent oversight of the conduct of government respecting Indigenous Rights as well as new methods of dispute resolution that include applications of Indigenous laws and processes
- new institutions that are independent of government and designed in partnership with communities that support the work of rebuilding their Nations and governments
- development of proper processes and structures between Canada and Indigenous governments for decision making, including in order to obtain free, prior, and informed consent.

Making these shifts internally within government and in partnership with Indigenous leadership will allow us to meet the goals of (1) moving from denial to recognition, (2) replacing conflict with cooperation, (3) removing the barriers to self-determination and the inherent right of self-government, and (4) creating the conditions for the cultural, social, and economic well-being of children, family, and communities. In short, it will support Nations to lead the work of transitioning from their current realities imposed by colonial structures to futures that reflect the priorities and visions of their peoples – the Nation rebuilding I talked of earlier. The tree.

Where rebuilt Indigenous Nations and governments are increasingly caring for their own people under their own laws – in other words, self-governing – and when Indigenous Nations are leading the way through their own institutions, Crown governments will need to respond and engage with the rebuilt Nations, to follow the lead. To this end, proper legislative and policy changes as well as new models of negotiations and agreements, developed in consultation and cooperation with Indigenous Peoples, must be about the federal government getting its house in order and supporting Nation rebuilding – and not in any way about regulating, limiting, or constraining the ability of Indigenous Peoples to exercise their rights, self-determine, and rebuild. Public officials must be bound to recognition standards and the legal control exercised by other governments over the lives of Indigenous Peoples pulled back.

Here, in BC, governments and Indigenous leaders have been dancing around legislative change to effect recognition for over a decade, and there is great opportunity for leadership – notwithstanding what other governments may or may not be doing. All of this is to say – we do have some experience and lessons learned from going down the legislative path here in BC. And we have learned from it. Yet, even with friendly governments and with progressive Indigenous leadership – change is always challenging. As the late Chief Joe Mathias reminded us during the constitutional talks on self-government in the 1980s – he said to "behold the turtle ... he moves forward when he sticks his neck out." The question remains today: Are we prepared to stick our necks out? I say let us stick our necks out. I am.

We must be audacious. We must do what is right and not look for a compromise between what is right and what is not – thinking it will propel us forward. Ultimately, we are speaking about shifts that are going to require multiple forms of action over many years. The turtle may move slowly – but it moves in a purposeful direction.

Not wanting to stick out your neck is directly related to overcoming our fears – which hold us back. In some respects, those fears are not surprising. While early patterns of relations between the Crown and Indigenous Peoples reflected a nation-to-nation relationship based on recognition, for far too long that has been ignored and lost, and many have become accustomed to the status quo. So, true nation-to-nation relationships have become an unknown change for many of us, and like everything in life, the unknown – and change – brings with it an element of fear.

Within government, when discussing matters of Indigenous Rights, one still often finds a seemingly disproportionate focus on "risk" – speculation that the sky may fall and an emphasis on the most severe, yet very remote, potential outcomes. These fears are reinforced by some voices in the public sphere that are opposed to aspects of the critical work of reconciliation. Thankfully, the influence of these voices is diminishing, but they still exist and remain a threat to progress.

But fear also holds Indigenous Nations back. Of course, many Nations across this province and across the country are advancing important change. They are rebuilding their governments, moving out of Indian Act structures and mindsets, and revitalizing and expressing anew their legal orders on the land. But this work needs to massively expand and accelerate. The fact is – recognition-based relationships cannot be grounded in structures and requirements imposed or propped up by the Indian Act; they need to be by and with Indigenous Nations that have self-determined their representative institutions and are exercising their self-government. Sometimes, fear holds some back from moving out from under the Indian Act.

As well, there are some Indigenous voices on the margins that will – purportedly in the name of upholding Indigenous Rights – critically oppose almost any effort to change, often relying on inflammatory rhetoric and misinformation that spreads fear, confusion, and mistrust. These voices, paradoxically, sometimes end up reinforcing the same outcome – inaction – that those who oppose rights recognition for Indigenous Peoples and reconciliation pursue.

As a former Regional Chief, I understand this. Among this group of Indigenous voices, one sometimes sees a tendency to what I would label as fundamentalism, which in any context is problematic. This includes the idea that there is not a place for Indigenous Peoples within a changed, rebuilt Canada. This group ultimately rejects both section 35 of the Constitution Act and the far-reaching judicial decisions regarding Indigenous Title and Rights and UNDRIP – this because both include, in varying ways, articulation of the relationship between Indigenous Peoples and Rights and the state and confirm the ongoing existence of the state: Canada. The rights recognition and Nation rebuilding we are advancing is within a strong, changed, and united Canada reflecting our system of multilevel government, cooperative federalism, and legal pluralism, including Indigenous jurisdictions and legal orders.

So, let me say this to all that want real change – courage is the opposite of fear. We need to be ever more courageous. We need the courage to realize that when making real change, not every future detail can be known; to understand that change has to be transformative while recognizing that we need to build on our success; to act in ways that take risks, because we know the status quo is not what anyone needs or wants; to not wait for others to lead. Generations of children and grandchildren have waited too long. We must lead the change ourselves.

Moving forward on track two and developing an appropriate rights-recognition framework is not just about the right process supported by the right substance. It is also about meaningful action along the way. Rather than delaying important lines of action while waiting for the necessary legislation to be developed, we should all be pushing forward.

Let me give an example of action I am taking in accordance with my authority as the Minister of Justice and Attorney General of Canada. From the day I was elected, I have spoken about the need to move the issues of rights recognition and reconciliation out of the courts. The goals of reconciliation and adversarial court processes are opposed to one another. This is why, some eighteen months ago, I issued internal direction to my litigators to operationalize the ten principles of the Government of Canada, adopted in July of 2017 in the context of Indigenous litigation. It is my intention to make this directive public before Christmas this year. This will reflect a principled approach and something I believe is important for transparency and accountability in the era of reconciliation.

That said, with respect to the directive, and as we all know, direction to litigators can only do so much. If we have arrived at that litigious place, then something has already gone wrong in the work we must do together. And ultimately, litigation direction and practices amongst all parties must change, not just the Crown's. But the directive is helping – I believe it will continue to help – in a range of ways, such as by changing specific aspects of the approach to litigation, simplifying and streamlining, reducing its adversarial nature, and making pleadings less offensive, and over time it will continue to change the culture that has been built up where litigation is often the norm instead of the exception. I hope to see multiple initiatives like this directive in the upcoming months that build momentum and trust as a reset takes place in how to get to proper recognition and implementation-of-rights legislation and policy.

And on that note, where do we go from here?

Forward, of course. We move forward without repeating mistakes, even if recent. We know what needs to be done, we know how to do it properly, we have governments and Indigenous Peoples aligned like at no time in history before, and we have a pressing urgency for transformative change that no one can deny. We need to act. There are no plausible or legitimate excuses for not making the shifts that are needed – to relations based on the recognition and implementation of rights. The remaining obstacles must be overcome.

I truly hope that the pace of real change begins to match the urgency of the ills we must address, on all tracks. I hope that regardless of whatever negotiation process you are in – the BC treaty process, recognition and self-determination tables, reconciliation negotiations – you innovate and accelerate to tangible outcomes in months, not years.

I would encourage that the kernels of innovation we see – including the Sechelt Foundation Agreement – are further advanced and made accessible so that Nations across the province and country can make real progress in a timely way. Everything ultimately boils down to this. Generations will look back and judge us on the actions we take right now – when we had the chance, when the stars aligned. When the stage was set for the long-awaited and fought-for change, did we fulfill our role and get it done? Did

On Obstruction, Denial, and Canada's Failure to Uphold the Rule of Law

Adapted from "From Denial to Recognition: The Challenges of Indigenous Justice in Canada," First Nations Provincial Justice Forum, April 24, 2019

As the Minister of Justice and Attorney General of Canada, I was committed to ensuring that our country's law and policies actually do change. As a foundation, that change must be consistent with the true meaning of recognition of rights and it must support the rebuilding of Indigenous Nations. Developing a province-wide First Nations justice strategy – in partnership with the provincial government – is so urgent, vital, and long overdue. It is work that so many of us in this room have fought so hard to advance. It is an important sign of the progress, collectively, that has been made that a joint provincial strategy is, finally, being drafted and implemented. And it will take us all.

Since I spoke to the leadership of British Columbia this past November, there have been a few developments. Things have changed a bit. Perhaps you are aware of them? Perhaps not fully unexpected but certainly an eventful time. Of course, when I spoke to you in November, I was still the Minister of Justice and Attorney General of Canada and the focus of my remarks then was about how true reconciliation requires courage, audacity, innovation, and a different approach to politics. Implied in this was how the challenges we were seeing in transforming laws and policies through a new recognition-and-implementation-of-rights framework illustrated that we need to govern and make decisions in new ways. Indeed, when I went to Ottawa in 2015, I carried with me the belief that how we govern ourselves as Indigenous Peoples carries important lessons for which Crown governments would do well to learn from. That belief is stronger today than ever before.

I want to offer a few reflections on the past few months (and the past few years) in particular, what lessons it might hold for the important work you are engaged in – transforming the relationship of Indigenous Peoples and the justice system. One of the developments over the past few months was that, finally, in my last act as Minister of Justice and Attorney General of Canada, I issued a directive about the conduct of the Crown in civil litigation with Indigenous Peoples. The directive lays out twenty guidelines aimed at shifting how litigation is conducted to be more respectful, recognition-based, and focused on promoting early settlement and measures to simplify legal proceedings. It is only a step, but it is an important one in the right direction.

In fact, this directive took a long time to be finalized and released. From the time I first announced we were preparing it back in July 2017, there were challenges – there were obstacles and some resistance. In order to move the directive along a lot of work was done, including testing our approaches, educating and training lawyers, dialoguing with experts (both internally and externally), and starting to make shifts in litigation practices that would come to be expressed formally in the directive. I am pleased that the work of implementing the directive within the Department of Justice is ongoing, and this must continue.

There were some within the establishment who were fearful that shifting from the norm of how the courts had been used against Indigenous Peoples would be a costly mistake; some who did not seem to understand that adversarial processes and the work of reconciliation are, and will always be, fundamentally in tension and typically at cross-purposes; some who – importantly – did not, and perhaps still do not, realize that uncertainty, conflict, and unpredictability arise because of the denial of rights, not because of their recognition.

But the reality that a directive on litigation from the minister was even needed speaks volumes to the much more foundational challenges we still face. The patterns of perpetual, expensive, and seemingly endless litigation we have fallen into is a symptom of a much deeper dilemma rooted in the history of our country and about how the law, and the justice system, has operated. Indeed, all of these terms – "justice system," "rule of law," "administration of justice," and others – have meant something starkly different for Indigenous Peoples than other Canadians. And it is that difference, that fundamental fact – that Canada's justice system has historically had a role in perpetuating injustice for Indigenous Peoples – that we are all working urgently to confront and change.

In my recent testimony before the Justice Committee on February 27, 2019, respecting the SNC-Lavalin controversy, I observed that "the history of Crown-Indigenous relations in this country includes a history of the rule of law not being respected, and I have seen the negative impacts for freedom, equality, and a just society this can have firsthand." I also stated that "we either have a system that is based on the rule of law, the independence of the prosecutorial functions, and respect for those charged to use their discretion and powers in particular ways – or we do not."

As these statements highlight, the rule of law is a principle intertwined with the highest values we uphold as a society – fairness, equality, nondiscrimination, upholding basic rights and fundamental freedoms, limitations on power, privilege, and undue influence. Values, when respected, applied, and upheld, are the critical foundation for inclusion, social cohesion, and democracy. When violated, there are significant risks of conflict, corruption, and the decay of the bonds and ties that allow diverse peoples to live and build a society together.

And, of course, as Indigenous Peoples, we have our own vital and important understandings and applications of the rule of law within our own traditions and legal orders. Within our diverse protocols and teachings and in how our laws are expressed – whether orally, in story, in art, or in writing – one sees how all of us have a responsibility to uphold the law and the wide range of mechanisms, customs, practices, and expressions that must be utilized to ensure that occurs. And within our oral traditions there is a paramountcy that we place on the truth. It is recognized that if we do not voice what is true, and pass that on, our society will fracture and erode. Speaking and truth telling can never be separated. This is a lesson that I believe Crown governments, and our national systems of politics, certainly can learn from.

With respect to Indigenous Peoples, the failure to uphold the rule of law in the history of Canada has been one significant factor in the history of Crown-Indigenous relations. We all know this too well. Historic treaties have been violated, the legal requirement for treaty making ignored, the direction for the recognition of the Indigenous relationship with the land in the Royal Proclamation of 1763 ignored, not to mention the imposition of an explicitly race-based, segregated, and unequal Indian Act system. I could go on. The examples are countless of how rather than the true meaning and standards of the rule of law, the history of Canada has seen these standards violated as it relates to Indigenous Peoples, and different standards, often grounded in racism and sexism, predominate. And the expressions of this pattern – of aspects of a double standard – continue right up until today, including in how Indigenous Peoples have been forced to "prove" the existence of rights enshrined in our Constitution in 1982 in ways that Charter rights, also enshrined in our Constitution in 1982, have not been.

Of course, when I became Minister of Justice and Attorney General, I had no illusions about this reality. I was not naive to the challenges but rather embraced them, and still do, despite all that may have transpired over the past few months. This is the reality I had fought to change alongside all of you and the reality I was committed to continuing to challenge in Ottawa. I believed then, and continue to believe now, that making the fundamental shift from relations based on denial to those based on the recognition of rights is urgent, imperative, and requires transformative, foundational changes to laws, policies, and operational practices.

It also requires Indigenous Nations to dynamically advance in tangible and innovative ways the work they – we – must do to rebuild the Nations and governments, to set priorities, organize as proper title and rights holders, reimagine and strengthen governance and their legal institutions and, very importantly, increase their capacity to develop, legislate, and enforce their laws.

This work should also be nonpartisan. This is not an arena of work conducive to political expediency, partisan games, cynical half-measures, or rhetoric not backed up with action. It requires boldness, courage, and a vigorous agenda for change from all of us. And where progress is being made, the momentum must be maintained and encouraged. This need for change is clear across the spectrum of political, economic, cultural, and social issues that we face as Indigenous Peoples and as a country. Nowhere is this clearer than in the relationship of Indigenous Peoples with the criminal justice system, and that is why I applaud the First Nations leadership in BC and the province for undertaking this joint work. Like all of you, I know people who from a young age have gotten stuck in endless cycles into and out of the criminal justice system. Breaking this pattern requires multilevel approaches – and I am glad to see how your strategy and work have been framed, that the ultimate goal of the strategy you are designing is to figure out the proper relations between self-governing and self-determined Nations regarding the administration of justice and the province's system, roles, and responsibilities in the administration of the justice system. This is the big picture. This is transformative. And also, I am glad to see that your strategy, in addition to systematically supporting achieving that vision, will pursue immediate and tangible changes to address the urgent challenges that arise regarding how Indigenous Peoples come into contact with the justice system and what transpires when they do.

Now, of course, there is still much work to be done with respect to the justice system – both the immediate changes and the bigger shifts in relation to self-governments. Let me reflect a bit on each. The types of immediate shifts that we focus on are well understood. We talk about restorative justice and the need to invest more in it, the implementation of the *Gladue* (1999) decision of the Supreme Court of Canada in sentencing, the formation and work of our organizations such as the Native Courtworkers, retraining those within the justice system such as prosecutors and the judiciary, the development of First Nations sentencing courts, changes to the jury system and bail processes, and so on (the need for C-75 on criminal justice reform to pass in this Parliament). All of these are vital and must be addressed in any strategy that is developed, as is the required work of supporting and investing in proactive programs and capacity building that help build healthier communities and provide new supports, as well as significant innovation in rehabilitative approaches within the corrections system.

To be clear, making these immediate and incremental shifts also requires some far-reaching changes to Crown legislation and policy – both federal and provincial – in the near term. For example, and it is no secret, I have long believed, and continue to believe, that mandatory minimum penalties perpetuate the crisis of the relationship between Indigenous Peoples and the justice system, and many of the immediate challenges cannot be as effectively addressed without the majority of MMPs being removed. To say it simply: MMPs feed the cycles of incarceration and overincarceration when our work needs to be to break those cycles. I firmly believe it is essential to moving forward and will continue to aggressively advocate for it.

But there remains significant unfinished work to accomplish before Indigenous Peoples have access to appropriate systems of justice, including Indigenous courts, so that they can enforce tribal and other laws as part of a multilevel system of evolving cooperative federalism that respects Indigenous legal orders. In fall 2018, I had announced plans for dialogues with Indigenous Peoples on how to advance this. Venues for such dialogue and work must carry forward.

Some areas for justice reform as an aspect of self-government and self-government implementation will be easier than others, and work is already underway, albeit not fast enough nor as well coordinated as it could be. We should have no illusions, though. Doing this work as it relates to the criminal justice system will be one of the hardest, if not the hardest, arena for change.

At Confederation, our criminal laws were confirmed as falling under federal jurisdiction in section 91 of our Constitution. From that time onward, the criminal law of Canada was built up, based on British law and with the passage of our first Criminal Code, in 1892. Of course, in parallel was the launching of another reality, the passage of the Indian Act, which regulated the lives of First Nations peoples and even made many aspects of our way of life criminal. In the colonial mindset, rather than subjects to be protected by the criminal laws of Canada, we were – and are – often objects to be protected from.

Rebuilding our own systems of justice, including our own courts and institutions, is vital to addressing this reality, and it is incumbent upon First

Nations to lead it. In order to be effective in the administration of justice, it is also important we recognize, as mentioned above, that foundations must be laid first. Moving out of the Indian Act and into systems and institutions built around our own constitutions is vital, as is building up the internal capacity for operating and growing those institutions. We need to turn our efforts to hard questions, including the ways in which we will choose to enforce our laws and how that enforcement will ensure the protection of all within our Nations, including, particularly, the most vulnerable.

We also have to think in very systematic and coherent ways about issues of transition from the existing justice system to one that includes recognized roles for Indigenous laws and systems. There will be no "one size fits all" model – it will necessarily have to look different and be attuned to how Nations are driving forward their work of rebuilding their governments and the priorities that are to be addressed. There will be issues, issues of economies of scale and financing, regulation and accreditation, and what has in the past been called the problems of "pan-Indianism," where we conflate different cultures under the general rubric of being "Indigenous."

Of course, this work moving forward also requires proper and basic Crown recognition of Indigenous Title, Rights, and Governments to take place. This is something that a little over a year ago I expected was going to happen imminently following the PM's historic words in the House of Commons. As you all know, this has not yet occurred, and I fear we may have temporarily fallen back into a less audacious and less meaningful conversation and mode of work that – while perhaps more comfortable – will not achieve the transformative space that is required. Of course, quarter-century-old policies need to be rewritten and negotiation approaches updated. But, ultimately, the lifeblood of colonialism is written in the laws of this country – including the Indian Act and how these laws deny our title and rights – and until the laws of Canada are changed to be based on recognition, fundamental patterns that need to be altered will remain with us. While steps forward are being taken, they are not happening as coherently, systematically, and quickly as is needed to set us on the proper and necessary path of recognition-based relations.

My fear, and disappointment, is that despite sounding the alarm, providing advice, pushing and challenging, sharing perspectives of lived Indigenous experience, providing a lens into the reality of being Indigenous, the federal government has fallen back, once again, into a pattern of trying to "manage the problem" with Indigenous Peoples and make incremental and limited shifts, rather than transforming the status quo. In my view, it is never appropriate or proper to have as a goal managing the challenges and the byproducts of colonialism. The goal must be to address the wrongs, change the patterns, transform the foundations – with all that we do framed in how to achieve those goals.

Again, this is where Crown governments have much to learn from us. We have experienced colonialism – we understand it – and we have the solutions. Despite the setbacks, I am confident that the work will not move away from our solutions if we remain vigilant. We have come so far. Indeed, although it was my expectation that the review of laws and policies that the federal government was to undertake in accordance with the ten principles that the government released in July 2017 would have happened earlier in the mandate, now, and at the eleventh hour, there is a push to revisit the so-called comprehensive land claims policies and self-government policies.

When it comes to the administration of justice – and as it relates to the work that the BC leadership is undertaking – I believe that it is through the revised policies on self-government, including the new fiscal policy with respect to funding self-governments, that the internal direction to the federal government will be given on the scope and extent of what the government sees as possible in this area. It goes without saying that we all need to ensure, with respect to justice and other matters of importance between Indigenous Peoples and the Crown, that our voices be heard, that these policies and laws are revised, and that they be based on recognition and not denial.

This brings me to some final observations that I would like to share that are about what the work of advancing reconciliation – which transforming the justice system is a part of – tells us about politics and the political culture that currently exists in Canada. To say it differently, reconciliation reminds us how desperately a different form of politics is needed in this country –

one with a new political culture. Reconciliation is a challenge that is vital for the survival and well-being of children, women, families, and communities across this country. To meet this challenge, hard choices, innovative actions, transformation in laws and policies, new understandings and attitudes, and new patterns of behaviour are needed. Long-term vision is needed; a willingness to think concretely about what the next generation needs and how to build that; the leadership to not take for granted the status quo of how things are done and to challenge them; the strength to know that this requires working across party lines, building support for bold approaches that can endure.

Over the last number of years – and especially over the past few months – I have heard from Canadians all across the country yearning for a new kind of politics. And in this regard, I think we, as Indigenous Peoples and leaders, have much to share and teach the rest of the country; about how, despite differences, our diverse teachings encourage us to strive to maintain a focus on achieving consensus; how, despite great obstacles, our legal orders and systems of justice have been maintained, and we continue to work to improve and advance them; and how we understand the roles and responsibilities that must be played within our governments and societies, how all of these roles are intended to contribute to advancing the well-being and health of all.

Doing work as Indigenous self-governments to develop our own systems for the administration of justice, while also reforming the current systems of justice that fall under the jurisdictions of federal and provincial governments, will be a major and essential contribution to the future of Canada. The overall success or failure of rebuilding Indigenous Nations in Canada, and the successful implementation of self-government, will, in large part, be determined by how well Indigenous Nations can enforce and adjudicate their own laws, as well as other governments' laws, and how well such systems will fit within the broader legal system in Canada.

As a last word, I just want to share that today, and every day, I remain optimistic and hopeful. Despite the challenges of the past few years and months, the path of progress and change is marching forward, and I think constructive work – led by Indigenous Peoples – is accelerating. We are seeing work being done together in ways that we have not seen before, and this is vitally important. This does not stop, nor is it dependent on one person or one voice. Of course, this is collective work that generations before us have carried forward, and which we are carrying forward now. The vigilance we must continue to have is to ensure that the work that is being done remains grounded in principles and standards and that the solutions being developed will truly result in honouring and respecting Indigenous laws, governments, and jurisdictions – whose ultimate goal is to improve the quality of life for our peoples – so we can care for our peoples, communities, and lands as we must. Indeed, as self-determination and self-government advances, we will see how it strengthens the well-being of Canada and all Canadians, including our social fabric, cohesion, and culture and economy.

Each of Us, in Our Own Way, Is a Hiligax̱te'

"Standing in Your Power, Using Your Voice," Feminists Deliver, June 6, 2019

I was asked to speak about the theme "Standing in Your Power, Using Your Voice." I know something about power, the power each of us can and does have and about using one's voice – I suspect we all do. I want to reflect on our power, and our voices, from four different but intimately connected perspectives: my own personal journey; the colonial experience with respect to Indigenous Peoples and changing power structures; my ongoing experience as a Member of Parliament and being the first Indigenous and only third female Minister of Justice and Attorney General of Canada, particularly around the work of "reconciliation"; and some final reflections on our country today and creating balance and a vision for our collective future.

I come from the Musgamagw Tsawateineuk/Laich-Kwil-Tach people of northern Vancouver Island, who are part of the Kwakwaka'wakw, also known as the Kwak'wala-speaking peoples. We are a matrilineal society, which means that descent is traced and property is inherited through the female line. We have hereditary Chiefs – always men – who are groomed for leadership. My father is the hereditary Chief of our Clan, the Eagle Clan. His name is Hemas Kla-Lee-Lee-Kla, which means "Number one amongst the Eagles, the Chief who is always there to help." He was given his name in a Potlatch, which is our traditional institution of government – one that we still practise. It is here where our names are passed down or given from generation to generation. It is where laws are made, disputes are settled, people are married, and where wealth is redistributed. In our Potlatch, the highest-ranking male leaders are called *Hamatsa.*

Rank is reflected in positions and names – which bring with them considerable responsibilities and obligations. My grandmother's name was Pugladee – the highest-ranking name in our Clan. Her name means "a good host" – a name that was given to my older sister, Kory, at the same time I was given my name. My name, Puglaas, means "a woman born to noble people." These names were given in a naming Potlatch at Gilford Island when I was five and my sister six.

My grandmother – Pugladee – ensured that both my sister and I knew our culture, our values, the laws of our Big House, and how to conduct oneself as a leader. We continue to learn. In our system, I am a Hiligax̱ste' – a role always held by women. One of my jobs is to lead my Hamatsa, the Chief, into the Big House. This role can be translated as one that "corrects the Chief's path." We show them the way, a metaphor for life and, in the Potlatch, symbolized in our rituals where, symbolically, the power of the Hamatsa is "tamed" and he is ready to be Chief.

In our traditional system of governance, there are no political parties; rather, we seek to govern through the principles of consensus, and the role of leaders is to seek that consensus. We meet, and while not everyone may agree on every aspect, we debate the issues and seek general agreement to help ensure that decisions are balanced, supported, and will be enduring – standing the test of time. We are expected to tell the truth and to speak up. Everyone speaks. While all this may sound idealistic to some who have never lived it, I assure you it is very real.

My grandmother used to joke with us that when it came to the respective roles of woman and men that the women were too busy and too important to be the Chiefs. But in all seriousness, we come from a communitarian culture. Everybody has a role to play in making our communities work well. The roles are very different but equally important in terms of ensuring the community functions the way it should. I call it balance. In fact, our whole system was about balance – between men and women, between Clans, and between Tribes.

I am fortunate to come from a strong and loving family. My grandmother and parents certainly raised me to be proud of who I am, to know where I came from, to believe in myself, and to recognize my rights and responsibilities. I was raised to lead from a very young age. My family instilled in me a sense of community and duty – that I had something to give back and to contribute, to use my skills and abilities, such as they are, to improve the quality of life for our people and others. In many ways, my role as Hiligaxste' has carried over into all aspects of my life. My upbringing, my education, my professional and personal experiences have all helped shape my worldview and the way I try to conduct myself.

Given our history as Indigenous Peoples, it is important to appreciate the context for how many of our leaders have felt compelled to comport themselves in their interactions within broader society. The colonial experience has not been easy for Indigenous Peoples, and this brings me to my second reflection on our power, our voices: the abuse of power, and the power imbalance, that has been a destructive part of the history of this country.

When the Fathers of Confederation came together in 1864 in Charlottetown and then again a month later in Quebec to lay out the foundation for Canada, Indigenous Peoples were not present – they were left out – this despite the early treaty making and the many political and military alliances made with Indigenous Peoples under the auspices of the Royal Proclamation of 1763. During the time of the Royal Proclamation, the colonial authorities actually recognized the power of the "Nations or Tribes of Indians" and the need to make treaties with them.

Unfortunately, after Confederation, Crown policy became one of assimilation – not mutual recognition – which, this week, the report of the National Inquiry into Missing and Murdered Indigenous Women and Girls constituted as "genocide." One of the most insidious of tools used to propagate the policy of assimilation, as you are all aware, was the Indian Act. The Indian Act is colonial legislation that the government enacted to govern and define the relationship between Indigenous Peoples and the rest of Canada. It imposed an alien system of governance that divided the 80 plus Tribes or Indigenous Nations into 630 plus administrative units called "bands." It established reserves and set out how the bands would be governed as well as who was, legally, an "Indian" and how this Indian status was passed on. The system was designed to ultimately enfranchise and assimilate "Indians." Among other racist policies of the government, it created residential schools to "remove the Indian from the child."

But for Indigenous women in Canada, the colonial experience was particularly harsh and still is – again, as the findings of the report of the National Inquiry into Murdered and Missing Indigenous Women and Girls clearly illustrate. The Indian Act, in turning Indigenous social and political systems on their head, often shifted the balance of power between men and women. For example, the Indian Act system does not acknowledge matrilineal heritage. By eradicating hereditary leadership structures, the Act abolished the central role of women in many of our Tribes in raising, teaching, guiding, and regulating Chiefs – for example, playing the role of a Hiligax̱ste' I mentioned earlier. Under the Indian Act, initially, only men could run and vote for the Chief and council. To make matters worse, if a woman married a man who was not registered as an Indian, she lost her status as an Indian and her right to be a member of the "band." Legally, she was cast out – if not physically. Conversely, a non-Indian woman who married an Indian man became a legal "Indian."

So, in many ways, the Indian Act distinctly suppressed women who had often been decision makers as well as providers in Indigenous societies and sought to remove us from public life. Indigenous women did not get the right to run for Chief or council and vote in band elections until 1951 – more than eighty years after Canada became a country. There have, of course, been some changes to this system, the result of advocacy, litigation, and shifts in public opinion. But the effects of marginalization and overt and covert forms of specific discrimination against Indigenous women remain with us.

Yet despite this history – this tragedy – what is so powerful today and so very encouraging and gives me great optimism is the demonstrated resilience of Indigenous Peoples and, in particular, Indigenous women, reflected in the integral role they are playing in the process of decolonization and the transition during this period of governance reform and Indigenous Nation rebuilding. It is women who are often in the forefront of advancing the process of true reconciliation with Indigenous Peoples –

which means confronting and ending the legacy of colonialism in Canada and replacing it with a future built on Indigenous self-determination, including self-government, through a rights-based and principled approach, which must include legislation and major policy shifts across government.

I think of the hundreds of women either living in Indigenous communities – living and working on reserve or living and working in our cities and who are not living in their ancestral homelands – who are leading the fundamental community development work that needs to take place to move through what I have often called the postcolonial door. Women are truly driving the needed governance and program reform to get beyond the Indian Act and other colonial institutions – something that became very clear to me in my work as BC Regional Chief of the Assembly of First Nations. Women are involved in rebuilding the institutions of good governance. It is the women who typically show up at community meetings and then roll up their sleeves to develop solutions and inclusive policy moving forward. Without minimizing the role of men, I truly believe Indigenous women are the forces of real change – of decolonization.

So while Indigenous women are making progress, politically and socially, we can and must do better – whether within the confines of the institutions we are transitioning away from or those that are evolving to replace them.

This brings me to my third reflection – on my experience over the past three and a half years as an Indigenous woman in national mainstream politics and as a Member of Parliament and as the Minister of Justice and Attorney General of Canada. Of course, I am very proud to continue to serve as the Member of Parliament for Vancouver Granville – just as serving as the Minister of Justice and the Attorney General of Canada for over three and a half years and Minister of Veterans Affairs was truly an honour.

With respect to Indigenous issues, as a proud Indigenous woman with the great responsibility of being Canada's first ever Indigenous Minister of Justice and Attorney General, I must say I felt a moral imperative to carry on the work of generations of Indigenous leaders before me and to help advance the necessary shifts that need to take place to transform the relationship between Indigenous Peoples and the Crown. I often said that I saw my appointment to that role not so much as a personal accomplishment but, rather, as a symbol of how far Canada has come but also of how much further we have to go. I still believe this – perhaps now more than ever.

We have seen real progress in patterns of thought, actions, and relations in the last decade. And we cannot diminish this fact. This is the fruit of the work and advocacy by Indigenous Peoples and many alongside. Even a decade ago, the work of reconciliation and justice, and addressing colonialism, was out of sight and out of mind for most Canadians. We have brought it out of the shadows. Much more has to be done, of course, but we are driving it forward. I know we will carry on advocating for the necessary transformative actions that will create the space – the foundation – for self-determination and the rebuilding of Indigenous Nations within Canada. We all need to be advocates in this work. It is the work I was doing as BC Regional Chief and as a council member in my own community before becoming Minister of Justice and Attorney General – a role I took, of course, very seriously, although at times it was a challenge and incredibly frustrating.

As I stated in a speech last year – when I was Minister of Justice and Attorney General – "in my own experience serving as the first Indigenous person to be Canada's Minister of Justice and Attorney General, I have unfortunately had it reinforced that when addressing Indigenous issues, no matter what table one sits around, or in what position, or with what title and appearance of influence and power, the experience of marginalization can still carry with you. But this does not deter me. It only makes my resolve stronger and more determined."

Apparently, this statement was truer than I imagined. Within a few months, I had made my very public, very proud, very liberating journey from the front bench of the governing party in the House of Commons to sitting in the furthest corner seat possible. This reality for essentially doing my job as an out-of-context Hiligax̱ste'.

This brings me to my last reflection on our country today – on creating balance and a vision for our collective future, if you like, some lessons learned and what more needs to be done. The events of the last few months have brought some further illustrations to light regarding women in politics and why we need more women in politics. Some of it is obvious: the standards one is held to and the double standards; how easy it is to label in racialized and gendered terms; that when a woman pushes back, stands up for principles, relies on their lived experience, or brings forward actual knowledge and experience they are easily and reflexively labelled as "difficult." Well, what I will say on this is that if doing those things is being "difficult" – I am proud to be difficult every day of my life.

And, of course, we see that a woman's lived experience is still often used against us, as a reason for marginalization, as a basis for blame. We see experience ultimately being used as part of a rationale for marginalization. Rather than upholding experience, using it as a lens to reconsider the norms of what one perceives or believes or chooses to uphold, we see a lack of reflection or, as it has sometimes been stated, that we "experience things differently."

In politics – where one is deemed difficult for speaking the truth, or for doing your job, or acting on principles (and then you are told you experienced it differently) – it is time for the culture of politics to change, and to facilitate this change, the systems and the rules need to be changed. And people, patterns of thought, and ways of relating need to change as well. To really make the change we need – for women to infiltrate politics and transform our political culture more than ever before, including confronting the divisiveness of partisanship, we need more independent voices to effect the transition. This is one of the major reasons I embrace being an Independent Member of Parliament – one who will continue to work hard and serve with this objective in mind.

I think it is fair to say that the current parliamentary system is structured in a way that impedes transformative change and that it breeds conflict and divisions rather than supporting lawmakers learning from each other. It favours and privileges norms and ways of doing business that make limited space for the lived experience and solutions that women, Indigenous Peoples, and other peoples in our society can bring forward. When I say this, I do so with respect and from the privilege of being in Canada, in a country where we are making progress.

So, when we consider where we have come from and where we are going, we need to consider context and where we are relative to others. There is, in reality, a continuum of progress with respect to the issues women face both in our country and globally. Internationally, Canada has a role to play, and we must lead by example. We can provide hope to so many. We must help to seek to eliminate barriers to equality everywhere – addressing the challenges that prevent women and girls from reaching their full potential. Women must be empowered to improve their own lives, and those of their families, communities, and countries. Whether here at home or abroad, simply put, empowering women and girls empowers humanity.

The recent announcement by my former colleague Minister Monsef of the investment to the women's Equality Fund is very significant. These investments by Canada will be a game changer for many. But that said – it does not buy us a hall pass or absolve us for our own transgressions or the need to do better. While Canada is a leader, this does not mean there is not room for improvement or that we can think that just because someone is empathetic or an ally that there may not still be issues. Being supportive cannot be used as cover for bad behaviour or where systemic problems ensure old ways still govern. On the contrary, it makes us have to do more. Yes, we may be further along the continuum of empowerment than for many parts of the world, but we are still not where we are ultimately going to end up if we keep on fighting.

Empowerment of women is, of course, one dimension of social diversity. Inclusiveness is a fundamental tenet or key value of democratic polities – so that all voices have a role in decision making – whether defined by gender, ethnicity, religion, region, economic status, age, or education. For me, it has always been a matter of common sense, not just morally but economically. Discrimination and inequality hurt economies, particularly in expanding knowledge-based economies like ours, where you need to maximize a nation's collective human potential. A country will never compete if they are not driving on all cylinders of their population.

There are things we can do in terms of institutional design and democratic reform to support the participation of women and other groups in public life – to effectively control the exercise of power and create balance. As a wise person once said, "Power tends to corrupt and absolute power corrupts absolutely." Controlling power is critical. And redefining power so that it is seen as valuing and upholding the strengths and capacities of each of us is critical. One thing I have come to appreciate in both Indigenous and non-Indigenous politics is that far too often people are seeking power for the sake of power itself, which is incredibly dangerous for society and, in particular, when governing in the complex world we live in. As in my culture, we have to "tame" the Hamatsa. Modern democracies require that those who govern are elected to do so for the right reasons and must be held accountable.

At the end of the day, it is the people who keep leaders and governments honest – which is, of course, much easier when the institutions for good governance are in place. But if people do not participate, we risk much. When the voice of the people is lost or truth is questioned, our governments are not held to account and, as a result, our individual opportunities as well as our collective prospects for a better future are severely diminished.

As both a woman and an Indigenous person, where our rights to participate in our systems of government were denied for so many years, I place great value, as I know you all do, on citizen engagement and ensuring broad participation in our political processes. So, in closing, let me leave you with this: please know and be confident that we all have a role to play in ultimately improving the quality of life in our communities – each role is equally important and is critical to ensuring that society functions as it should. Always speak the truth, be guided by principles and integrity – it will never steer you wrong. Yes, there will be challenges and setbacks but we all have a voice, and we need to support each other in using our voices, and together we have the power to change the world.

Each of us, in our own way, is a Hiligaxste'. We each have an important role to play in guiding the path forward and helping our societies find balance and flourish. Together, we can correct the imbalance we experience in society and help amplify the voices and power of those who have been muted for too long.

Gilakas'la.

ACKNOWLEDGMENTS

I would like to thank the many people that have helped me on my journey and made invaluable contributions to this book. There are, however, simply far too many to acknowledge by name – people who have inspired, supported, and assisted me over the years, including those who have challenged me and provided thoughtful guidance.

I express my thanks and pride for the generations of Indigenous Peoples – past, present, and future – from coast to coast to coast – who have shown resilience, strength, and steadfast determination to build a more just Canada. This work continues as we collectively seek to deconstruct the colonial legacy and embrace an era of recognition and reconciliation – one where our Nations are rebuilt with practising and thriving cultures.

In my personal journey, I must acknowledge the part played by the three most important and beloved women I have had in my life: my feisty and determined grandmother Pugladee (Ethel Pearson), who provided my cultural grounding; my kind and generous mother, Sandra Wilson, who continues to provide me with unconditional love and support and ensures I remain connected; and my sister, Kory Wilson, who is my closest friend and confidant and with whom leadership was learned and shared. To my indomitable father, Hemas Kla-Lee-Lee-Kla (William Lane Wilson), who taught me how to live in two worlds, to be an advocate: I thank you for your strength, integrity, and unwavering commitment to the advancement of Indigenous Rights and the law. And to all the other Knowledge Holders who have shared your wisdom about our teachings and our ways – *Gilakas'la*.

Thank you to all who encouraged and supported me to take on greater leadership roles by seeking political office, whether within the Indigenous world or within the political mainstream and whether locally, regionally, or nationally, from Chief Brian Assu, Chief Maureen Chapman, former Chief Ralph Dick, Grand Chief Edward John, Grand Chief Stewart Phillip, Miles Richardson, and Jack Weisgerber (who in a very frank moment encouraged me to run in my first election ... Jack, my friend, do you remember what you said?) to Prime Minister Paul Martin (whom I first met at one of our BCAFN Assemblies years ago when I was talking about governance and have stayed connected with ever since) and Prime Minister Justin Trudeau (who first asked me to run to be an MP and subsequently asked me to serve as MOJAG). And, of course, to the constituents of Vancouver Granville for your ongoing support in allowing me to proudly serve as your Member of Parliament.

As for my speeches over the years, many people come to mind – whether it be discussing ideas, undertaking research, or preparing or reviewing drafts. Some of you are from my time at the British Columbia Assembly of First Nations, some from my time at the Department of Justice and as an MP, and some from all three. From all three: Dr. Roshan Danesh, thanks for constantly challenging me in our work – I am grateful for the day our paths crossed; Lea Nicholas-Mackenzie, we have been through so much together, and you remain my barometer and dear friend; and Whitney Morrison, from a once young and amazing BCAFN intern to a trusted adviser – Gilakas'la. At the BCAFN, thank you to Debra Hanuse (remember our first days, Deb ...), Courtney Daws, Angie Derrickson, Alyssa Melnyk, and to the BCAFN Board of Directors and my Elder adviser, Hereditary Chief Robert Joseph. At the national office of the AFN, thank you to the executive members I had the opportunity to work with over the years and to Karen Campbell and Jennifer Brennan for your work on the governance file. At the Department of Justice, thank you to everyone who worked in my minister's office, specifically Jessica Prince and Gregoire

Webber and the many able speech reviewers, Katie Black, Emma Carver, David Taylor, and Keith Smith. And to all the hard-working and committed public servants in the department, I say thank you. To my first deputy, William F. Pentney, I will always be grateful to you for your wisdom, compassion, and friendship. To Deputy Minster Natalie Drouin, thank you for always supporting our transformative vision, and to the one and only Geoff Bickert, my former assistant deputy attorney general – thank you for your calm guidance, wit, and commitment (and for the sign that still sits on my desk). To all those who have worked with me in our Vancouver Granville constituency offices – particularly Christine Faron Chan and Bernard Higham – I am grateful to each of you every day. And to the Honourable Jane Philpott, thank you for your ongoing commitment to reconciliation, for your able review of many of my speeches, and for your friendship.

I know there are many more people that I have not mentioned specifically, but thank you.

In getting this book to print so quickly, I am very grateful to the exemplary team at UBC Press, from my incredible editor, Lesley Erickson, through to the acquisitions, production, and marketing staff, notably Randy Schmidt, Nadine Pedersen, Carmen Tiampo, Holly Keller, Irma Rodriguez, Frank Chow, Cheryl Lemmens, Laraine Coates, and Kerry Kilmartin. Thank you, President Santa Ono, for the constant support you have shown this alumnus, for being so open to the idea of this book, and for connecting me with the amazing Melissa Pitts, director of UBC Press.

Most importantly, to my husband, Dr. Tim Raybould, thank you for your fierce opinions and passion and, most of all, for your love and support in this journey. The writings in this book span much of our marriage, and I know I could not have done any of this without you. To our nieces and nephew, Kaija, Kaylene, Kadence, Jasmine, and Miles – you collectively are my inspiration.

Before I close, I must also acknowledge my community of We Wai Kai (Cape Mudge) and all our friends and family – you know who you are. And thank you for always being who you are when we are back in the village and in the place where, in fact, many of the words in this book were penned.

A NOTE ON TERMINOLOGY
AND THE SPEECHES

Over the ten years that spanned my time as BC Regional Chief, Member of Parliament, and Minister of Justice and Attorney General, I gave many talks to diverse audiences. The ones that appear in this book represent only a small sample, selected to highlight the five main areas of my thinking when it comes to what needs to be done to chart a new course for true reconciliation in Canada.

The wording of the speeches has not been changed, but they have been edited to serve the purposes of this book. In addition to making the style for spelling, capitalization, and punctuation consistent, greetings have been removed, as have direct remarks to the audience. In some cases, material was cut to avoid repetition (referred to as "adapted"); in others, only an excerpt of the original speech was included. No material has been added. To aid the reader, abbreviations have been spelled out, and references to "the Prime Minister," when unclear, have been recast to include a surname.

Over the past decade, the terminology used to refer to Indigenous Peoples – First Nations, Inuit, and Métis – in Canada has changed. When I was Regional Chief, the acceptable term was "Aboriginal Peoples," which is embedded in section 35 of Canada's Constitution and section 25 of the Charter. In the last few years, however, it has been replaced by "Indigenous

Peoples," the term favoured in the United Nations Declaration on the Rights of Indigenous Peoples and by Indigenous Peoples. This shift is reflected in the speeches. As most Canadians now understand, the term "Indian" was imposed on Indigenous Peoples by colonial agents and by the Indian Act. But it is still appropriate to use "Indian" when referring to the status of people under the Indian Act. The style used in this book conforms to Gregory Younging's *Elements of Indigenous Style: A Guide for Writing by and about Indigenous Peoples*.

To see the full text of my speeches, along with other documents referred to in these pages, see the online compendium at https://open.library.ubc.ca/search?q=*&collection=ubcpress&creator=Wilson-Raybould,%20Jody.

CASE LAW AND
LEGISLATION CITED

CASE LAW

Calder v British Columbia (AG), [1973] SCR 313, 1973 CanLII 4 (SCC).
Delgamuukw v British Columbia, [1997] 3 SCR 1010, 1997 CanLII 302 (SCC).
Haida Nation v British Columbia (Minister of Forests), [2004] 3 SCR 511, 2004 SCC 73 (CanLII).
McIvor v The Registrar, Indian and Northern Affairs, 2007 BCSC 827, [2007] 3 CNLR 72; *McIvor v Canada (Registrar of Indian and Northern Affairs)*, 2009 BCCA 153, [2009] 2 CNLR 236.
Musqueam Indian Band v Glass, [2000] 2 SCR 633, 2000 SCC 52 (CanLII).
R v Gladue, [1999] 1 SCR 688, 1999 CanLII 679 (SCC).
Taku River Tlingit First Nation v British Columbia (Project Assessment Director), [2004] 3 SCR 550, 2004 SCC 74 (CanLII).
Tsilhqot'in Nation v British Columbia, [2008] 1 CNLR 112, 2007 BCSC 1700 (CanLII); *Tsilhqot'in Nation v British Columbia*, [2014] 2 SCR 257, 2014 SCC 44 (CanLII).

STATUTES

First Nations Commercial and Industrial Development Act, SC 2005, c 53.
First Nations Fiscal and Statistical Management Act, SC 2005, c 9.
First Nations Land Management Act, SC 1999, c 24.
First Nations Oil and Gas and Moneys Management Act, SC 2005, c 48
Water Sustainability Act, SBC 2014, c 15.

BILLS AND THEIR OUTCOMES

Identified by bill number (C = House of Commons; S = Senate)

Bill C-3, *An Act to promote Gender Equity in Indian Registration by responding to the Court of Appeal for British Columbia Decision in McIvor v. Canada (Registrar of Indian and Northern Affairs). Gender Equity in Indian Registration Act,* 40th Parliament, 3rd Session, SC 2010, c 18. Passed December 15, 2010.

Bill C-27, *An Act to enhance the Financial Accountability and Transparency of First Nations. First Nations Financial Transparency Act,* 41st Parliament, 1st Session, SC 2013, c 7. Passed March 27, 2013.

Bill C-31, *An Act to amend the Indian Act,* 33rd Parliament, 1st Session, SC 1985, c 27. Passed April 17, 1985.

Bill C-69, *An Act to enact the Impact Assessment Act and the Canadian Energy Regulator Act, to amend the Navigation Protection Act and to make consequential amendments to other Acts,* 42nd Parliament, 1st Session, SC 2019, c 28. Passed June 21, 2019.

Bill C-75, *An Act to amend the Criminal Code, the Youth Criminal Justice Act and other Acts and to make consequential amendments to other Acts,* 42nd Parliament, 1st Session, SC 2019, c 25. Passed June 21, 2019.

Bill C-262, *An Act to ensure that the Laws of Canada are in Harmony with the United Nations Declaration on the Rights of Indigenous Peoples (United Nations Declaration on the Rights of Indigenous Peoples Act),* 42nd Parliament, 1st Session. Third reading May 30, 2018.

Bill S-2, *An Act Respecting Family Homes situated on First Nation Reserves and Matrimonial Interests or Rights in or to Structures and Lands situated on those Reserves (Family Homes on Reserves and Matrimonial Interests or Rights Act),* 41st Parliament, 1st Session, SC 2013, c 20. Passed June 19, 2013.

Bill S-6, *An Act respecting the election and term of office of chiefs and councillors of certain First Nations and the composition of council of those First Nations,* 41st Parliament, 1st Session. Second reading and referral to committee in the House of Commons June 17, 2013.

Bill S-8, *An Act Respecting the Safety of Drinking Water on First Nation Lands.* Safe Drinking Water for First Nations Act, 41st Parliament, 1st Session, SC 2013, c 21. Passed June 19, 2013.

Bill S-212, *An Act Providing for the Recognition of Self-Governing First Nations of Canada (First Nations Self-Government Recognition Act),* 41st Parliament, 1st Session. First reading November 1, 2012.

INDEX

The Honourable Jody Wilson-Raybould, PC, QC, MP,
also known by her initials JWR and by her ancestral name
Puglaas, is a lawyer, advocate, and a proud Indigenous
Canadian. She is a descendant of the Musgamagw
Tsawataineuk and Laich-Kwil-Tach peoples, which are
part of the Kwakwaka'wakw or Kwak'wala-speaking peoples,
and she is a member of the We Wai Kai Nation.

Throughout her career, Ms. Wilson-Raybould has built a
strong reputation as a bridge builder between communities
and a champion of good governance, justice, and accountability. She was elected as the Member of Parliament for the new
constituency of Vancouver Granville on October 19, 2015.
On November 4, 2015, she was appointed the Minister of
Justice and Attorney General of Canada, making her the first
Indigenous person to serve in this portfolio. She then served

---

Photograph by Andrew Meade, *The Hill Times*

as Minister of Veterans Affairs from January 14, 2019, to February 12, 2019.

Prior to entering politics, she was a provincial Crown prosecutor in Vancouver and later served as an adviser at the BC Treaty Commission, a body established to oversee complex treaty negotiations between First Nations and the Crown. In 2004, she was elected as Commissioner by the Chiefs of the First Nations Summit.

In 2009, Ms. Wilson-Raybould was elected BC Regional Chief of the Assembly of First Nations, where she devoted herself to the advancement of First Nations governance, fair access to lands and resources, as well as improved education and health care services. She was re-elected as Regional Chief in 2012 and served until 2015, holding responsibilities for governance and nation building on the Assembly of First Nations National Executive. Ms. Wilson-Raybould also served two terms as an elected Councillor for the We Wai Kai Nation between 2009 and 2015.

An active volunteer in the community, Ms. Wilson-Raybould has been a director for Capilano College, the Minerva Foundation for BC Women, the Nuyumbalees Cultural Centre, and the National Centre for First Nations Governance. She was also a director on the First Nations Lands Advisory Board and Chair of the First Nations Finance Authority.

Ms. Wilson-Raybould lives in Vancouver and is married to Dr. Tim Raybould.